D1530847

MORE THAN WORDS CAN SAY

MORE THAN WORDS CAN SAY

PERSONAL PERSPECTIVES ON LITERACY

Copyright © 1990 McClelland & Stewart Inc.

All rights reserved. The use of any part of this publication reproduced, transmitted in any form or by any means, electronic, mechanical, photocopying, recording, or otherwise, or stored in a retrieval system, without the prior written consent of the publisher – or, in case of photocopying or other reprographic copying, a licence from Canadian Reprography Collective – is an infringement of the copyright law.

CANADIAN CATALOGUING IN PUBLICATION DATA
Main entry under title:

More than words can say : personal perspectives on literacy

Initiated by Canadian Organization for Development through Education.
ISBN 0-7710-2166-6

1. Literacy. 2. Canadian literature (English) – 20th century.* I. Canadian Organization for Development through Education.

LC149.M66 1990 302.2'244 C90-093695-9

Printed and bound in Canada

Thanks to Friesen Printers for donating printing and binding time.

McClelland & Stewart Inc.
The Canadian Publishers
481 University Avenue
Toronto, Ont.
M5G 2E9

More Than Words Can Say was originally conceived by CODE as a means to commemorate International Literacy Year (1990), to promote awareness of the importance of literacy, and to support literacy projects in the developing world.

Through the generous support of the contributors, McClelland & Stewart Inc., and the Canadian Booksellers' Association, the book provides a vehicle through which the importance of literacy is underlined. Moreover, proceeds from the sale of the book will be matched by the Canadian International Development Agency (CIDA) and used by CODE to provide books, paper for indigenous publishing, and educational equipment in 40 countries in Africa, the Caribbean, and the Pacific.

For more than three decades, CODE has been meeting vital literacy needs in Third World countries by supporting organizations that encourage people to learn and retain literacy, technical and daily living skills. Today, CODE is Canada's largest book-sending agency and one of the largest in the world. CODE is an international leader in the fields of literacy and indigenous publishing in developing countries.

CODE would like to thank Avie Bennett, Chairman and President of McClelland & Stewart Inc., whose personal endorsement of this project from the beginning has meant that these printed words will now provide the gift of literacy to thousands of grateful recipients.

CODE would also like to acknowledge the enthusiastic and generous response of all the contributors as well as McClelland & Stewart's Douglas Gibson, Don Sedgwick, and Ellen Seligman, whose constant professional support ensured that *More Than Words Can Say* would provide a creative contribution to the world of literacy. Special thanks must also be given to Knowlton Nash, Honorary Chairman of CODE, for his untiring efforts on behalf of CODE.

Elizabeth Kane

Elizabeth Kane
Director, Public Education
and Fundraising, CODE

CODE

CONTENTS

MORE
THAN
WORDS
CAN
SAY

BRUCE MACAULAY

Ever since Knowlton Nash was a child turning out the neighbourhood newspaper, he has been involved with the news. He worked with weekly newspapers and magazines and joined British United Press in 1947 as a reporter and editor in bureaus in Toronto, Halifax, and Vancouver. In 1951, he went to Washington, D.C., as Director of Information for the International Federation of Agricultural Producers, and in 1958 became a freelance Washington correspondent contributing to CBC Radio and TV, as well as to numerous magazines and newspapers throughout Canada. In 1969, Nash returned to Canada to head all CBC television information programming, and in 1978 became the well-known anchor of "The National."

Knowlton Nash is the honorary chairman of CODE. His books include the best-selling *History on the Run* and *Prime Time at Ten*, and his next book, *Diefenbaker and Kennedy*, is to be published in 1990. Nash was made an Officer of the Order of Canada in 1989. He lives in Toronto with his wife, Lorraine Thomson.

KNOWLTON NASH

Foreword

Books of stories; books of history; books of learning. They line the bookshelves of the nation with unimaginable riches for all our hungry minds.

When I go to a bookstore, I'm filled with the anticipation of a kid in a candy store, tempted by so many choices. And it's true for most of us as our eyes range along the shelves of literary delights. Sometimes, though, I pause in my scanning of book titles, as images come flashing into my mind of a one-room school shack in the Bogota slums or a thatched-roof shanty in Fiji's Yasawa Islands housing the village library.

I was doing a TV documentary on the crises of Latin America and accidently found myself in a tiny Bogota school called "Parque du Canada" where 80 youngsters shared four school books. The school had been built thanks to the generosity of a group of Toronto business people, and a policeman, who acted as a teacher in his spare time, had found the four books which were the sum total of reading material for the youngsters. Those four books seemed something almost magical for the youngsters, and I can still see in my mind's eye one skinny little cherub fingering one of the books with reverential wonder and care.

In the Fiji shanty, they had more books – maybe 30 in all – but villagers were allowed only to read them at a spindly table by an open window in the makeshift library. As in Bogota, there was a reverence here, too, shown by the young mothers and old men whom I watched coming to finger the words as they slowly read line by line.

When I snap back from my reveries to the cornucopia of reading material on our Canadian bookshelves, I realize how incomprehensibly lucky we are, and how empty life would be without the books, the magazines, and the newspapers that give us insight and delight, information and knowledge.

It's hard to imagine a world without books and yet for so many millions, that is exactly their world. Thirty years ago, a request for a set of encyclopedias came to several Toronto teachers from an overseas school. From that simple beginning, the Canadian Organization for Development through Education (CODE) was born. Today, thanks to contributions from concerned Canadians, the Canadian International Development Agency, Canadian publishers, paper companies, and others, CODE sends upwards of one million books a year to third world countries, and it also provides paper so they can produce hundreds of thousands of their own books.

In Jamaica alone, for instance CODE has provided over the years not only books, but paper for more than eight million textbooks. In Tanzania in 1989 CODE committed $278,000 to help produce 180,000 chemistry and biology textbooks and teacher's guides.

CODE, with generous co-operation from McClelland and Stewart and the Canadian Booksellers' Association and many others, has produced this book of anecdotal stories and memories on the joys of reading, and learning to read, to mark the United Nations International Literacy Year 1990. This book is a salute to literacy by some of Canada's outstanding writers and cartoonists. We're grateful to them not only for their contributions to this book, but for the joy and enrichment they have given all of us through the years with their creative genius.

The objective of the International Literacy Year is to begin to shrink the number of people who can't read. There are nearly a billion adults around the world who can't read or write and hundreds of millions of youngsters who don't have the chance to learn. CODE's objective is to help the oldsters and the youngsters to learn by reading.

Literacy is the cement out of which the fundamental building blocks of progress are made. A book is more than paper and ink when it can teach people how to save lives and build homes, teach job skills and enrich minds. A book can be the beginning of everything.

JACK RODICK

Terry Mosher, a.k.a. Aislin, is the editorial-page cartoonist of the *Montreal Gazette*. Mosher, forty-six, was born in Ottawa.

Aislin cartoons are syndicated throughout Canada, and have appeared in many prominent publications around the world. The recipient of many awards, Terry Mosher was the youngest person ever inducted into The Canadian News Hall of Fame, in 1985.

Terry Mosher lives in downtown Montreal with his wife, two daughters, and nine cats – seven at home, two in his studio. *The Lawn Jockey*, his twentieth book, was published in 1989.

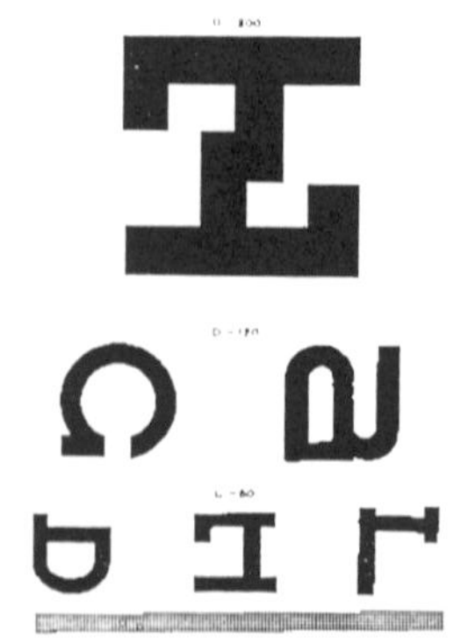

AISLIN 89

JAN ZARZYCKI

Sandra L Birdsell

Successful fiction writer, scriptwriter, playwright, and filmmaker, Sandra Birdsell was born in Morris, Manitoba, and moved to Winnipeg in 1967. She has won numerous awards for her writing, including the Gerald Lampert Award for new fiction and the National Magazine Award for short fiction. In 1986, she was named one of Canada's Ten Best Fiction Writers in the "45 Below" competition. Her two books of short stories, *Night Travellers* and *Ladies of the House*, were highly praised. Her first novel, *The Missing Child*, was published in 1989, and received wide critical acclaim. Sandra Birdsell lives in Winnipeg, where she is working on her next novel.

SANDRA BIRDSELL

I Used to Play Bass in a Band

I met Terry this summer one sweltering night as I sat out on the deck visiting with a friend. I had been away from Winnipeg for two years and Roger, who operates a travel agency in the area, summarized the changes in the neighbourhood. The neighbourhood: the rubbing of shoulders on Westminster Avenue of professional people along with the indigent natives and the poor on their way to the Agape Table, the funky and most of the city's artists, all living within several blocks in an area in Winnipeg which is referred to as the "Granola Belt."

Sounds from the front street echoed between the houses, the sounds of parties in the making in the clink of empty bottles inside beer cartons. A person riding a bicycle darted by in the lane and I saw the flash of long copper-coloured hair as the rider passed through the light of the streetlamp. "And then there's Terry," my friend sang softly under his breath and was about to say more when we heard the sound of tires skidding as the bicycle came to a halt. Terry, straddling the bicycle, walked backwards into view and stopped beside a pile of boxes across the lane. Their contents, the remainder of a garage sale held earlier in the day, had already attracted much attention. One of our lawn chairs may have squeaked or perhaps the movement was as minute as the blink of an eye, but Terry sensed our presence and veered away from the stack of cartons. Roger called a greeting and then explained that Terry often dropped by the agency to browse but more than often to talk his ear off.

Terry shielded his eyes against the glare of the streetlamp and peered into the yard. Then he stood up and simply walked free of his bicycle, letting it drop to the ground. He appeared to be all limbs and had the awkward lope of a young animal as he entered the yard, calling his greeting in breathless run-on sentences.

"Rog, hey Rog, how're you doing, eh? Haven't seen you in ages, man, how're you been? I checked out your lead? Medi Equip? Wanted me to work in a spray booth. No ventilation, just masks, eh. I told them no way. I'm not putting my lungs on the line for the minimum. So, how you been, eh?" His voice has a disarming quality to it, yet urgent too. Like that of a cat entering a yard in the morning after a long night of prowling and not being able to decide whether it wants to be fed or fondled.

Roger introduced us. I was intrigued by the contradictions in Terry's appearance: the suggestion of fragility in his much-too-thin body, the audacious "screw the world" kind of message on his tee-shirt which belied the tremor of vulnerability in his anxious smile. The tilt of his khaki beret, the stylish paisley scarf knotted at his waist, were at odds with his scuffed and almost shapeless cowboy boots. A knapsack dangled at his side. He towered above us, casting a lean shadow across the lawn. He was like the street, I thought. A combination of all the people who passed by my house.

"Your soffits are rotting," he said. "If you don't get them replaced you'll end up with water damage in the ceilings on the second floor." He said he couldn't help but notice the loose boards each time he passed by. I didn't know whether to be annoyed or grateful for the information. I sensed Roger's uneasiness when I invited Terry to join us and offered him a cold drink.

When I returned from the house, Terry had helped himself to a cigarette from Roger's package and jostled a handful of nuts he'd scooped from the bowl on the table. Beside the bowl was a pamphlet. He said it was for me, that he wasn't in the business, not to worry, eh. He wasn't trying to sell me anything but in his estimation, this company's line of roofing supplies was the best. He liked my house, he said; like all the houses in the neighbourhood, it had character. I asked him if he lived in the area, then, but instead of answering, he shifted in his chair suddenly and pointed out a garage across the street. "Used to be a livery stable, far out," he said and did we know that once all the houses along here burned coal? "Fossil fuel, imagine," he said. "I can imagine the shapes of fossils drifting up the chimneys."

"Aha," I said in answer. Not long ago when I had gone walking in the night I had passed by a young woman with a dreamy, serene smile. She'd said good evening and then warned me to take care because the cats were flying in the sky. I said aha then, too.

Terry stooped to rummage in the knapsack planted between his feet. "Picked this up today," he said. The book was a colourful compact guide to fossils, the kind often sold in museum gift shops. He thumbed through it. I asked him if he was interested in geology.

"Adapt or die," he said, "except for the cockroach. Paleontology is the study of fossils," he read. "Yeah, I'm interested." He closed the book and placed it on the table in front of him. "You know the painting, *Starry Night*?" he asked. He'd seen it in a retrospective of Vincent van Gogh and what he'd really like to do, he said, was paint like that. "Instead of stars," he said and nudged at the book with a long bony finger, "I'd like to paint the sky full of trilobites swimming in a tropical forest." I told him I had once lined up for half a day outside a gallery in Paris to see the painting in a show of van Gogh's work and I thought it was impossible to improve on a van Gogh sky. "Oh wow," he said, "you've seen it? Oh wow." He shook his head at the wonder of it. So was he, Terry, an artist, then?

"Yeah," he said with the same nervous shift in his body. "That and music, eh. I used to play bass in a band." I tried not to smile. I thought his statement would make a great title for a story. "I used to play bass in a band" neatly summed up the lives of several young people I had met recently.

Terry set his empty glass down on the table between us and leaned forward. "Tell me," he said, "do you think van Gogh was crazy?"

Well, I wondered, hadn't the man been treated by a psychiatrist and for a time confined?

Terry was quiet for several moments. It seemed to me that his sharp features had become less fox-like and softer. "I don't know whether he was or not," he said, "but that's what most people say. That he was crazy. But what I think," he said, "is that when van Gogh painted, he was in a different state of consciousness."

Roger replied wryly, yes, drunk as opposed to sober. Terry's expression grew strained and his voice appealed for our patience, to let him finish what he'd begun to say. "Hey, Rog, no, listen, man." I sensed he was accustomed to being dismissed. "Hey Rog, why do you think there are so many crazy people in the world?" he asked, using the trick of a question to make Roger pay attention and then going on to say what he wanted to say. "Because," he said, "because so-called crazy people can't conform to the common idea of what is reality."

Which was what? Roger wanted to know. "The reality determined by the first scientists," Terry said. "The cause-and-effect guys, everything can be counted and measured. The notion that we live in a rational and predictable universe." There was no way, he said, that scientists would ever be able to construct a working model of the brain where these other realities existed. Van Gogh hadn't been crazy at all. He'd just given in to his own sense of reality. "You know that I think?" he said. His sharp features grew more animated. "I think the reason why we only use such a small part of our brain is because we've adopted a caveman theory on the idea of what is sense and what is nonsense."

He tapped his forehead and grinned. "Tunnel thinking," he said. "Van Gogh had an alternate sense of reality. Probably, all artists do."

"You?" Roger asked.

Terry laughed and lifted his slender hands as though to push the notion away. "Hey man, I'm not that stupid," he said. His wide grin lit up his eyes. "What would you say if I told you that I can actually see trilobites in the sky? You'd get nervous and I might end up with a chemically induced sense of your reality. So I tell you that I imagine I see them. Adapt or die," he said. "There's no way I'm cutting off my ear, man."

We stood on the sidewalk in front of the house. Terry said he wanted to check out the buskers in the Village. In the light of the streetlamp his face appeared pinched and rather pale. I noticed that his teeth were pitted with decay. He pushed off and joined the flow of traffic, the music, the other cyclists. Roger explained that he'd begun to see Terry in early spring. That Terry had slept in a bus shelter on the corner and, he suspected now that it was warmer, along the river bank. "Alternative sense of reality," he said and laughed. "Where does he get those things?" He added that he didn't believe Terry to be a user of drugs.

While the noise of a full-blown party doesn't bother me, I am often awakened in the night by the small sounds, footsteps in the back lane or the creak of a gate. I lay awake listening to the sound of stealth, someone rummaging through the boxes across the lane. I went to the window and saw Terry standing below in the light of the streetlamp. He was without a shirt now and I could see the outline of his ribs beneath his shallow chest. He cradled a book in his hands and turned the pages carefully, as if it were a delicate object. He stopped paging then and stood as though transfixed, leaning into the text. I watched, mesmerized by his intense concentration, a spell cast, and I was unable to move away. The neighbourhood, I, and the night became invisible as we stood, holding our breaths outside of Terry's world.

ANNE MARCOUX

Neil Bissoondath's first collection of stories, *Digging Up the Mountains*, earned him admiration both in Canada and abroad. His acclaimed first novel, *A Casual Brutality*, was published in Canada, the U.S., the U.K., and in translation in Germany.

He was born in Trinidad, in 1955, and emigrated to Canada in 1973 to attend York University. Since graduating, he has taught English and French. His stories have been broadcast on CBC, and have been published in *Saturday Night*. A new collection of stories, *On the Eve of Uncertain Tomorrows*, will be published internationally in the fall of 1990.

Neil Bissoondath divides his time between Montreal and Toronto.

NEIL BISSOONDATH

Choose a Book, Choose Another

The floor is of hardwood polished to a dark sheen. It is warm, silken under the bare skin of my legs. A clean morning light shines in through the open window above, the air still cool, not yet hardened by the blazing tropical sun.

On the floor in front of me lies a book, hardcovered in cloth of faded green, the corners soft and whitened. It belongs to my mother and I have taken it from the radio stand, the second tier of which serves as her bookshelf. I open the book, turn the pages, the yellowed paper thick and floury to the touch. The print is so large, a rich black, the lines well-spaced. Every tenth page or so, the text gives way to a drawing, simple sketches of Roman statues, and it is here that I pause, to examine these renderings of headless or armless men and women.

I am intoxicated with the light, the air, and the comforting mustiness that rises from the pages.

This is one of my earliest, and fondest, memories. I must have been four or five at the time and in the early stages of discovering the pleasure that was to become an addiction, that was to shape my life both personally and professionally.

I have no idea what the book was about – Roman history? Roman Art? I have no recollection of having actually read it. But neither the drawings nor the text was the true fascination. The attraction was, at that young age, more tactile than that. What, more than anything else, remains with me are the texture and feel of the book, its smell of old paper and old ink and glue crackling to dust. The book – its sheer physical presence – was an icon of things that I could not at the time put into words.

Reading came early and easily to me. Favourite gifts received were books, books, and more books. Returning from an extended trip to Europe, my parents brought me the tales of King Arthur and the knights of the round table; there were other presents, but it is the only one I remember, as I remember it was Jules Verne that comforted me after their departure; as I remember, three or four years later, an aunt taking me to a bookstore a week before Christmas and telling me, "Choose a book," and when I had, "Choose another," and another, and another. I was breathless with excitement and the difficulty of choosing from among the many that I coveted – and heartbroken that I had to wait a week before taking possession of them, gift-wrapped and beribboned.

My mother's library grew with the years. She read constantly and widely, of fiction and nonfiction, of the obscure and the popular, often working her way through two or three books at the same time. It was through her that I discovered some of my favourite writers, and from her too that I learned literary possessiveness, determining early on not to lend books, for they were not precious to other people, were infrequently returned – and how could you in good conscience surrender to the uncaring hands of others objects that seemed to embrace you with their worlds, that stirred your deepest dreams and fantasies? My quintessential picture of my mother is of her stretched out on her bed or a sofa, one book held open before her eyes and another bookmarked beside her.

Like my mother, I was never without a book – folk and fairy tales, *The Iliad* and *The Odyssey* for children, The Hardy Boys, *Treasure Island*, *Kidnapped*, countless others. A book or two accompanied me everywhere, on visits to relatives, to the beach where I would occasionally cause resentments by preferring the company of the printed word to that of cousins and fishing rods. How many hours did I spend at the local library, devouring stories, drinking in illustrations, seeking treasures among the rows of neatly stacked shelves? Mine was by no means a solitary childhood. I had friends, relatives galore, played cricket, tennis. But reading, escape to other worlds, other adventures, was essential to me. If Trinidad was small – and it felt small even then – access to the wider world was never distant, was as close as an unread book. Bereft of books, I would have felt isolated and vulnerable. Cheated.

When, at the age of 18, I came alone to Toronto, it was once more reading – late nights with Dostoyevsky, Tolstoy, Mishima, Hemingway, Solzhenitsyn – that eased me through the initial loneliness. My book collection grew quickly, and as it did, so did my sense of belonging, as if the pleasures of adult literary discovery were somehow planting me solidly into this new land.

There is, I am told, a certain inevitability to my becoming a writer. I am related to writers, come from a family that has long treasured in one way or another literary expression. The realization, when I was nine or ten, that I did not have to be a doctor or a lawyer or a businessman, that writing was itself an honoured and not impossible profession – I had, after all, an uncle who earned his living producing these objects that so enchanted me – was like a revelation, one I held tightly onto through impatient years of schooling and teaching.

This love of reading – and of writing, its logical extension – has given shape and purpose to my life, has anchored me through its pleasure and its instruction. It's chilling to wonder who I would be, where I would be and what I would be doing without it.

My mother died suddenly in November 1984, almost six months before the publication of my first book. Part of the enduring sadness is that we were both denied the anticipated pleasure of the moment when I would give her a copy of my own book. But that, I suppose, is – like the best fiction – life. Some time afterward, her books, numbering in the hundreds, were given to me by my family. They are now on my bookshelves, intermingled with mine. The green-covered book is not among them; it has long disappeared. But the books I have written are there, along with the books of her father and brothers. On my bookshelves, then, in a way more vivid than photographs, is a family continuity created by shared passions.

Words, sentences, books: so much more than simple pleasure, so much the very heart of life itself.

PHOTOGRAPH BY CARLOS

Harry Bruce

Born and raised in Toronto, Harry Bruce moved to Nova Scotia in 1971 and has lived there ever since. He is the author of nine books, concentrating mostly on popular history and biography. His latest book, *Down Home: Notes of a Maritimes Son*, was published in 1988.

Harry Bruce is perhaps best known for his personal journalism and numerous articles in major Canadian magazines, spanning the past twenty-five years. His father, journalist Charles Bruce, won the Governor General's Award for poetry, and each of his three children is involved in journalism. He lives in the house where his father was born in Port Shoreham, Nova Scotia, with his wife, Penny.

HARRY BRUCE

The Dark Hole of Illiteracy

Aware that more than two billion people can neither read nor write the simplest message in any language, the United Nations has declared 1990 International Literacy Year. I've been reading for half a century, and it is as hard for me to imagine what it's like to be illiterate as it is to imagine what it's like to be mute, blind, and deaf. Being illiterate must be life imprisonment in a dark hole.

I recently read out loud to two dozen grade six children from a tough neighbourhood in north end Halifax, and though they were not illiterate, neither were they book lovers. My reading embarrassed them. They weren't sure why they were there, and as I droned on, they ceaselessly whispered and sniggered.

But when I read to grade six children in the city's south end, where the cats were fat, the reaction was totally different. These kids were with me. They really listened. They got my jokes. They knew that books were important, and writers worth hearing.

Since the rudeness of the poor kids annoyed me, I cut their reading short, and invited questions. One boy, who had the cockiness of a gang leader, asked how much money I earned, and I replied, "Well it varies, but I usually make a few hundred dollars a week." This amazed him and his friends. They found it incomprehensible that anyone could sell words on paper for hundreds of dollars.

He wanted to know how I had become a writer. "My father was a writer," I said, "and maybe that had something to do with it. Our house was full of books, and by the time I was eight I was crazy about reading."

Another murmur of astonishment rippled through the class. Eyes rolled in disbelief. A house full of books? A boy who was nuts about reading? Could this possibly be true?

I now realized I'd been wrong to be annoyed. These youngsters lived in dwellings in which books were as rare as jacuzzis, or Alex Colville serigraphs. Some of their parents might have been illiterate. I felt these kids were doomed to become chambermaids, hookers, street fighters, and crack dealers.

Their dismal future, I was sure, had something to do with the fact that they had never known houses in which people loved books, and never would. They were denizens of Halifax's own third world.

All my life, I had been luckier than they. Before I could read, my mother read to me *The Jungle Book* and *Just-So Stories* by Rudyard Kipling, and I can still hear her drawling that magnificent description, "The great gray-green, greasy Limpopo River, all set about with fever trees." She also introduced me to Toad, Rat, Mole, and Badger of Kenneth Grahame's *The Wind in the Willows*.

When I was seven, I paid my first visit to a small, warm lending library in central Toronto. I took out four books in the morning, read them at home, and went back in the afternoon for more. (They had big pictures, and big print.) That dusty little institution smelled of well-fingered bindings, and like the three neighbourhood movie theatres, it became a beloved hangout of mine. It loaned me books about wolves, sharks, bears, birds, trains, ocean liners, planes, bush pilots, explorers, soldiers, smugglers, cowboys and Indians.

I read *Treasure Island*, *Robinson Crusoe*, *With Clive in India*, *Dale of the Mounted*, *Twenty Thousand Leagues Under the Sea*, *The Call of the Wild*, scores upon scores of lesser yarns, and as I grew older, the works of John Buchan, H.G. Wells, Ray Bradbury, Shirley Jackson, F. Scott Fitzgerald, Ernest Hemingway, William Faulkner, John Steinbeck, the British poets of World War I, Robert Frost, e.e. cummings, T.S. Eliot, Dylan Thomas. . . .

Each writer gave me the dazzling richness of a world that he or she had created. I was still a boy when I learned to revel in the invented kingdoms of writers. Long after my mother told me to turn out my light and go to sleep, I'd pull my bedcovers over my head, and read by flashlight.

I did this for years, which may be why I've had to wear glasses for four decades. But it may also be why I can do something as miraculous as selling words on paper for hundreds of dollars.

Remembering the way sleepiness and the weak flashlight beam made my eyes burn under the covers, I know precisely what Halifax-raised broadcaster Robert MacNeil meant when, in his recent book *Wordstruck*, he talked of "the discovery that words make another place, a place to escape to with your spirit alone. Every child entranced by reading stumbles on that blissful experience sooner or later."

The tragedy is that hundreds of millions of children are not entranced by reading. They can't read, and never in their lives will they stumble on that blissful experience. They are in the hole.

BRIAN SUMMERS

Born in Toronto in 1903, Morley Callaghan attended Trinity College at the University of Toronto and subsequently graduated from Osgoode Hall Law School in 1928. He worked as a journalist at *The Toronto Star*, then called *The Toronto Daily Star*. In 1928, Morley spent a year in Paris, where he met celebrated literary figures like Hemingway, Joyce, and Fitzgerald.

His short stories have been published in: *A Native Argosy* (1929), *Now That April's Here and Other Stories*, *Morley Callaghan's Short Stories*, and *The Lost and Found Stories of Morley Callaghan*. Morley Callaghan's first novel, *Strange Fugitive*, was followed in 1934 by the major novel *Such Is My Beloved*. In 1963, he published the memorable book, *That Summer in Paris*. His latest novel, *A Wild Old Man on the Road*, was published in 1988.

He received the Governor General's Award for Literature in 1952 for *The Loved and the Lost*.

As well as the Governor General's Award, Morley Callaghan has received the gold medal of the Royal Society of Canada, the Lorne Pierce Medal, the City of Toronto's Medal of Merit, the Canada Council Medal, the Molson Prize, and the Royal Bank Award. In 1982, he was appointed a Companion of the Order of Canada. Morley Callaghan lives in Toronto.

MORLEY CALLAGHAN

"My Love for Miracles of the Imagination"

One night back in the 50s when television was making its first big impact, my friend Ralph Allen, at that time editor of *Maclean's*, said to me: "We'd better all start learning to handle pictures and images. From now on there'll be less and less reading of stories or anything else. In fact, we should be worrying about whether reading is on the way out."

I simply couldn't believe this. We argued. I wasn't quite sure why I was so utterly positive I was right, and I remember that on the way home I tried to figure it out, and now I think I did.

I saw then that watching television and reading are two entirely different experiences. You can love one and hate the other. You can get so drugged by television that you can't take the time to read anything. Reading becomes an effort. Television is a spectator sport.

What you are watching is all outside you and goes on even if for long stretches you are falling asleep. I watch a lot of television; I get comfortable in the chair and half the time I'm daydreaming, I'm thinking of something else, half hypnotized, mentally inert, but comfortable, very comfortable.

But reading – this vastly different experience – requires work from me. My inner eye comes to life. If it's a story I'm reading, the figures come to life on the screen of my own imagination.

Language, just words, is making the miracle. The greatest wonder of humankind is probably the development of language, and the second wonder, growing out of the first one, is learning to read; letting another man or woman who is maybe dead, or maybe 10,000 miles away, reach into one's imagination and create a vivid, moving world.

A man sits alone with a book, the whole world around him grows silent, a voice so secret it can't be heard, just felt, is whispering to him and leading him deep into the world of the greatest wonder and power – his own imagination.

To this day I remember the first long story I ever read. It was called "The Fall of the House of Garth." I was nine years old. The book was a cheap pulp horror story. I forget who gave it to me. But I'll never forget my rapt attention or how the figures were dancing around so wildly in my imagination.

I had discovered reading and what it could do for the free, fresh imagination and how it could enlarge the whole world of wonders, and as time passed and I grew much older, and though I read and read a thousand works, I think I was always looking for some writer, some book that would give back to me the fresh imagination of a child.

Ripeness is all, freshness is all – how do you get this

stuff? Where do you get it? And looking back, and looking around at others, I can see that the person who keeps stimulating his or her imagination, stretching it like a rubber band through the visions of others coming through lovely reading, never grows old in the heart.

I had a friend, a Russian Jew who had some serious optical problem. He wore glasses with very thick lenses. I asked him what had ruined his eyesight. He said that when he was a boy in Russia his parents had been very poor. He had had to work hard. His mother always got him to bed very early and turned out the light. But he would have a flashlight in the bed, and pulling the covers over his head, he would read by the flashlight.

He read the stories of Chekhov, then book after book of Tolstoy before his eyes finally went on him. Looking back on it, he couldn't regret the damage to his eyes, he said. In his little tent under the covers his beam of light had opened up new worlds, worlds he would walk in the rest of his life; worlds that put him far beyond his poverty-stricken home and made him aware of lives far different than his own.

As this man knows, now that he is middle-aged, you don't have to have money, or go to college, to find the magic of reading bringing new planets swinging into your ken. It happened in a big way for me, though, in my first year at college. Up to that time I had been reading for fun all the boys' books, then Dumas and the Three Musketeers, and so on.

And then one day, sitting in the Hart House library, I picked up a short novel by a Russian I had heard of, Dostoyevsky. The little book jarred me; I knew I was being forced to look at things in a new way. I had got my first taste of real writing. I was excited. I had to find other writers who had other upsetting visions. For me they became the great writers. I remember being curled up on a couch in that library, reading Flaubert's *Madame Bovary*. I should have been at a lecture. But I had to get to the end of the book. Yet I did not want the book to end.

Well, Flaubert, in one of his letters to the great Russian Turgenev, said that there was nothing new for a writer to say, but there had to be new ways of saying the old things. All my life I've had this in mind as I read and read, and when I find a writer who has his own way of saying things, I get excited; another angle of life; again the new planet.

I used to find that sometimes I was not in the mood for new things, and then I would read as I watched television – just relaxing. At one time I read all of Agatha Christie, and all of the tough mysteries of Raymond Chandler. I'll read any newspaper, too. The newspaper is in my blood. I have to know what's going on.

But back in my mind, always is the longing to read something that will not only stir me, but give back to me the unspoiled freshness of imagination that I had as a child when I read "The Fall of the House of Garth." The trouble is I'm a professional writer, and even when I'm reading a good book now, my critical intelligence is getting too often in the way of my imagination.

Another bad thing I have to guard against as I grow older is finding it easier to read nonfiction than fiction. A book like Barbara Tuchman's *A Distant Mirror* about the European fourteenth century can completely absorb me.

I don't have to use my imagination at all. Ah, that worries me!

Then I look around eagerly for good new story writers. I now know I have one simple rule for knowing if they're good. They're good if they make me want to write. Or excite my imagination.

I know what it's like for a man who finally comes to realize that he has let his imagination wither and die and has grown old in the heart. He knows he is half dead. I saw it one night in a man I knew who was with me at a big party.

He was a very successful executive and only 55. He was having trouble with his wife. Sitting on the stairs he called, "Morley, sit with me. I want to tell you something." Holding my arm tight, he said desperately, "When I come home at night I'm tired. The rat race. I eat, I have a drink, I pick up *Time* magazine. I read three pages and fall asleep. . . ."

He had started to cry. Tears were running down his cheeks. "I know I'm a little drunk," he said, "but I used to read all the time. When I was at college I was crazy about Katherine Mansfield and Virginia Woolf. I read Sherwood Anderson, I read . . . oh, what happened to me?"

I often think of this man, particularly when I'm about to fall into a sweet little sleep, watching television.

"My Love for Miracles of the Imagination" first appeared in *The Toronto Star* (December 1986). Reprinted by permission of the author.

JOHN MEDLAND

June Callwood

June Callwood was born in 1924 in Chatham, Ontario. She was a prominent magazine writer in the 1950s, particularly for *Maclean's*, and in the 1960s became an activist for such social causes as homeless youth and battered women. She has continued writing, and, in addition to ghostwriting the autobiographies of numerous American celebrities, she has published various works, including *The Law Is Not for Women*, *Portrait of Canada*, *Emotions*, *Twelve Weeks in Spring*, and *Jim: A Life with Aids*. She became an Officer of the Order of Canada in 1986, and a member of the Order of Ontario in 1988.

For twenty-four years, she was vice president of the Canadian Civil Liberties Association. She holds eight honorary degrees, is president of the Canadian Centre of PEN International, a bencher of the Law Society of Upper Canada, and the former chair of the Writers' Union of Canada. June Callwood is also the founder and former president of Casey House Hospice, Nellie's Hostel for Women, and Jessie's Centre for Teenagers. She is married to sportswriter Trent Frayne.

JUNE CALLWOOD

Why Canada Has to Beat Its Literacy Problem

Carole Boudrias shudders when she remembers the time she almost swallowed Drano because she thought it was Bromo. Even more painful to recall is the time she mistook adult pain-killers for the child-size dose and made her feverish child much sicker.

"When you can't read," she explains, "it's like being in prison. You can't travel very far from where you live because you can't read street signs. You have to shop for food but you don't know what's in most of the packages. You stick to the ones in a glass jar or with a picture on the label. You can't look for bargains because you can't understand a sign that says 'Reduced.' I would ask the clerk where is something and the clerk would say, aisle five. Only I couldn't read aisle five. I'd pretend that I was confused so they'd lead me right to the shelf."

Carole Boudrias is able to read now, at last. She's a 33-year-old single parent who lives with her five children in a handsome townhouse on Toronto's harbourfront and holds a steady job. But her struggle with illiteracy is all too vivid in her memory. "You can't get a job," she says earnestly. "You can't open a bank account. You have to depend on other people. You feel you don't belong. You can't help your children. You can't help yourself."

Six years ago when her oldest child started school, the boy floundered. Because he had been raised in a household without books, print was strange to him. He would point to a word in his reader, that classic, endearingly silly *Dick and Jane*, and ask his mother what it was. She was as baffled as he, so he'd check with his teacher the next day and that evening would proudly read the new word to his mother. She began to absorb the shape of the words he identified. She found she could recognize them even days later.

That was astonishing. As a child she had been labelled mentally retarded and confined to "opportunity classes" where reading wasn't taught. She grew up believing that she wasn't intelligent enough to learn. Nevertheless, she *was* learning. The vocabulary of words she could read in her son's reader was growing. She began to think maybe the experts were wrong. Then, one miraculous day, she realized she was learning to read even faster than her son was.

"My son was my first teacher," she grins. She had never allowed herself to believe that it was possible that she could learn to read. She hadn't even tried: no one whose life is made up of poverty and failed relationships is ready to take on, voluntarily, the potential for another defeat, another kick in the self-esteem. She hesitated a long time but the evidence was persuasive – she was beginning to read. Her welfare worker had always been kind, so she summoned the nerve to ask her where she could find help.

That lead her to Beat the Street, a program that helps people who are illiterate for all the reasons that befall sad children: unrecognized learning disabilities, emotional stress, too many schools, scorn and belittling, terror, bad teachers. She was linked with a volunteer tutor, and they came to admire each other deeply.

"Now I can read, I can read books, anything. I can write. In English *and* French."

Carole Boudrias has written a book, *The Struggle for Survival*, which tells of her tortured childhood lacerated with incest and violence, and her triumphant recovery from illiteracy. Last summer she was the poet laureate of the annual golf tournament hosted by Peter Gzowski, the beloved and respected heart of CBC Radio's *Morningside*. He has befriended the cause of literacy in Canada and over the past four years has raised a quarter of a million dollars for Frontier College, one of the first organizations in the country to tackle the problem of illiteracy.

"Learning to read," Carole Boudrias says quietly, "was like a second birth, this time with my eyes open. Before I could read, I was a blind person."

Canada has nearly five million adult citizens who are described as functionally illiterate, which means that they can recognize a few words, such as washroom signs and exits, but they can't read dense print at all. They can't decipher directions, for instance, or application forms, or warnings on labels. The world of newspapers, posters, advertising, books, menus, banking, recipes, and instructions-for-assembly that literate people take for granted is barred to them; they live a life of bluff, anxiety, embarrassment, and isolation.

A good many Canadians are as profoundly illiterate as Carole Boudrias was. People who meet illiterate adults are struck by the similarity of their textural experience. All of them liken the inability to read and write with being disabled or chained in a prison. Edwin Newman, a U.S. broadcaster who writes about language, calls illiteracy "death in life."

The sense of being caged and blinded is not morbid fantasy. People who can't read may be able to walk freely but they can't go far. Subway stops rarely have pictures to guide them and the destinations bannered across the front of buses and streetcars are meaningless. If they ask for directions, well-intentioned people tell them, "Go along Main Street to Elm and turn left." Consequently, they must travel by taxi or stay home, though they usually are the poorest of the poor.

Almost every job, even simple manual labour such as street-cleaning, requires an ability to read. Personnel managers don't take kindly to people who can't fill out an application, or when asked, can't spell their own addresses.

The divide between the literate and illiterate has never been wider. In this half of the century North America has become a world of forms and documents and instructions, written warnings, posted rules, leaflets, and vital information circulated in brochures. Two generations ago, illiteracy was prevalent but not such a great disadvantage. Someone functionally illiterate could fake it through an entire lifetime and still hold a good job. Employment skills were acquired by watching someone else; apprenticeship was the accepted teacher, not two years in a community college.

Today inability to read is a ticket to social segregation and economic oblivion. A poignant example is the skilled house-painter who turned up one day in the crowded quarters of the East End Literacy Program in Toronto. He said he wanted to read. The counsellor asked him, as all applicants are asked, what he wanted to read. "Directions on paint cans," he answered promptly. "I'm losing jobs. I can't read how to mix the colours."

Many who are illiterate can't read numbers. When they are paid, they don't know if they are being cheated. Because she couldn't fill out bank deposit slips, Carole Boudrias used to cash her welfare cheque in a storefront outlet which clips poor people sharply for no-frills service. To pay for goods, she would hold out a handful of money and let the cashier take what was needed – and perhaps more, she never knew. Once she would have been short-changed $50 she could ill afford if a stranger who witnessed the transaction hadn't protested.

The common emotional characteristic of people who can't read is depression and self-dislike. All feel at fault for their situation: with few exceptions, they went through school with bright little girls exactly their age who leaped to their feet to recite and smart little boys who did multiplication in their heads. Everyone else in the world, it seemed, could learn with ease; for them, even C-A-T looked a meaningless scribble. Teachers called them stupid; worse, so did other children.

"Stupid" may just be the cruellest word in the language. It consumes confidence, on which the ability to learn relies. Seven-year-olds having trouble with reading will frolic at recess with an edge of glee; 11-year-olds who can't read have bitter faces and scarred souls.

Loss of hope for oneself is a descent into desolation without end. It causes men to rage in fury and women to wound themselves. People who can't read come readily to view themselves as worthless junk, and many feel they must grab what they can out of life and run. Canada's prisons are full of young men who can't read. The Elizabeth Fry Society estimates that close to 90 per cent of the women in Kingston's infamous prison for women are illiterate.

Because Canada has five million people who can't read, the political shape of the country and the priorities of governments are not influenced greatly by the needs of the poor. Since illiterates are effectively disenfranchised, the political agenda is written by the more powerful. Candidates rarely find it advantageous to uphold the causes that matter most to Canada's illiterates – an end to homelessness and the need for food banks, welfare payments that meet the poverty line, and better educational and job-training opportunities. Few votes would follow any politician with such a crusade. The electorate that can't read won't be there to ruffle the complacent on election day.

Their silence costs this country severely. Education is free in Canada because it was recognized that democracy isn't healthy unless all citizens understand current events and issues. Five million Canadians can't do that. Voters, most of them literate, choose candidates who help their interests; those who don't vote, many of them illiterate, by default get a government that does not need to know they exist.

The result is a kind of apartheid. The government has lopsided representation, which results in decisions which further alienate and discourage the unrepresented. The gap between the haves and have-nots in Canada is already greater than at any time in this century, and widening. Urban apartment houses are the work places of crack dealers, the streets are increasingly unsafe, and households have installed electronic security systems. The poor, if asked, would have better answers than guard dogs. The best, most lasting responses to crime and addiction and violence are literacy programs, coupled with job training and full employment.

Schools are in disgrace, with a failure rate of fully one-third of all high school students. A soup company with such a record would be out of business in a day. The educational system has managed to exacerbate the class differences which are developing in this country. Canada's millions of illiterates went through school the required number of years, give or take time-out for truancy, illness, running away from abuse, and confinement in detention homes. These human discards, identified promptly in the first years of elementary schools, will ever after drift around disconsolately. They are surplus people, spare parts for which society has no use. Unless there is a war.

Carole Boudrias is working on a project, Moms in Motion, to help young mothers to get off welfare rolls. She says to them, "What do you want?" They reply, "To go back to school."

Another chance. Five million Canadians need another chance. Maybe they can become literate, maybe they can become healed and whole. What a lovely goal for the 1990s.

BAY WEYMAN

Matt Cohen

Matt Cohen was born in Kingston, Ontario and educated at the University of Toronto. He is the author of several novels, including the critically acclaimed quartet the "Salem novels" and most recently, *Nadine*. His work has been translated into several languages.

He is well known for his short story collections, including, *The Expatriate*, *Café Le Dog*, and *Living on Water*. A new novel will be published later this year. Matt Cohen and his family live in Toronto.

MATT COHEN

"With An Introduction by the Author"

It was a hot summer night, and through the open window of his study the author could hear cats howling like a chorus of flatulent critics waiting for his next mistake.

He looked at the sentence he had just written. It was terrible. Also, it was bound to get him into trouble with the press, a sin his publisher always warned him about – among others. Why was he writing it? he asked himself, not for the first time. Of course he knew the answer. (He always knew the answer). He tore the page out of his typewriter and inserted a new piece of blank paper. Not for the first time he wished he had been the one to invent the idea of blank paper. Talk about arranging you own funeral! "People are interested in what you think about your own stories," the editor said.

The author brushed a few flecks of imaginary dust from the special writing suit his mother had given him for Chanuka 36 years ago and loosened his tie. He put his feet on the desk and imagined himself lighting a cigar. Then he imagined himself throwing his Panama hat – the one he had used to protect himself while saving orphans from piranhas (but that is another story) – on the floor. Then he imagined himself imagining a knock at the door.

"Hello?"

"Greetings." A beautiful woman entered the room. She had dark hair falling to her shoulders, burning eyes, long shapely legs that climaxed in brightly painted toenails.

"Who are you?" asked the author. Of course he already knew the answer. (He always knew the answer). She was the perfect client, an escapee from a detective novel he had started a few months ago. The novel had been too good to publish so he used it to pad his wastebasket.

"I'm not your mother," the beautiful woman said enigmatically, "no offence intended."

"None taken," said the author. In fact he was taken totally aback. All these years he had thought he was only writing books. Never in his wildest dreams had he dared to hope that his creations might – as his English teacher once put it – "live and breathe."

"As I live and breathe," said the beautiful woman, "I never thought I would have the privilege of meeting you. Do you know that I have read every one of your books?"

"Twice?"

"That would be asking too much," she said, making herself comfortable on his desk and lighting a black Russian cigarette. She opened a file drawer and threw her still-burning match on top of his latest manuscript.

Then she reached out, took off his panama hat (the one

he had bought in Paris in order to disguise himself as a Mexican), and threw it on the floor.

"What are you writing these days?" she asked, leaning over his typewriter and looking at the blank page. "Any chance of a part for me? I hated the way you called me Louella-May, the last time. No wonder you tried to throw me out."

"What would you like me to call you?"

"Call me what you like, sweetie – except for Louella-May – but my name is Monica." Monica was so close to the author he began to wonder if it would be incest to borrow a drag from her Russian cigarette. Then Monica touched him. She stretched her slender fingers out towards his neck and, with a practised motion, undid his tie so that it slid helplessly to the floor.

The author felt his writing suit getting itchy.

"What did you say you were working on?"

"Oh nothing, really. Actually, I was just supposed to be doing a little introduction for my book of short stories."

Monica kissed his neck. "What a cute little topic. I just *love* literature." She plunged her hands down his unbuttoned shirt. "What's the angle?"

"That's just the trouble," the author groaned, trying to keep Monica's hair out of his eyes as she nibbled at his ears. "I don't have one. The editor told me I should write about the difference between novels and short stories."

"You're kidding! I had exactly the same topic in grade twelve English!"

"You did?"

"It was an incredible. I just wrote my little heart out and

then the teacher failed me. I had to go back to his office every night for a month."

"Gee," said the author, "you're even worse at this than I am."

"Don't worry, honey, at the end of the month he gave me an A+."

"An A+!"

"And you know what?" Monica whispered rhetorically.

"No."

"I had the strangest premonition before I came to see you tonight, so I read that essay over."

"Gee," said the author, "did you happen to remember it?"

"Of course, darling, I remember everything. I'm your muse."

"Okay," said the author, as Monica leaned into him. He had always heard it would be this way, that when his long apprenticeship was over the muse would finally arrive and then, perched on his shoulder, would whisper the sweet nothings of art into his ear.

"Don't type this," Monica whispered, "but before we start I want you to know that I feel very, very sincere." She gave him a passionate kiss that left him no doubt about her intentions. "How do you like that?"

"I like it."

"Good," Monica said, "good." A sudden calm descended and the author realized that up until this moment he had been not in his own safe study but in the dark of wild

Africa, waiting outside the tent of Ernest Hemingway while he composed *The Snows of Kilimanjaro*. "I think I could whip you into shape," Monica said, "if you know what I mean."

"Give me an example."

"Okay. I'll dictate, you write." She kicked off her shoes and flicked a burning ember from her cigarette so that it skittered across his floor like a radioactive June bug. *"It was a hot summer night, and through the open. . . ."*

or

"Okay," Monica, "time to start filling that cute little page. I'll dictate, you write." From outside the window the noise of howling had increased; Monica kicked off her shoes and flicked her still-burning cigarette into the dark and querulous mouth of the night. "You see, honey, a novel is like one of those boring old-fashioned marriages, but a short story is a one night stand. . . ."

"With an Introduction by the Author" is from the Penguin Books edition of *Café Le Dog* (1985). Reprinted with the permission of the author and Penguin Books Canada. *Café Le Dog* was originally published by McClelland & Stewart Inc. (1979).

PETER PATERSON

Robertson Davies was born and raised in Ontario and was educated at Upper Canada College, Queen's University, and Balliol College, Oxford. He has had three successive careers – first as an actor with the Old Vic Company in England, then as publisher of *The Peterborough Examiner*, and most recently as a university professor and first Master of Massey College at the University of Toronto, from which he retired in 1981. He now holds the title of Master Emeritus.

He is one of Canada's most distinguished men of letters, with over thirty books to his credit, among them several volumes of plays, as well as collections of essays, speeches, and *belles lettres*. As a novelist he has gained fame, far beyond Canada's borders, for his Deptford trilogy: *Fifth Business*, *The Manticore*, and *World of Wonders*, and for his last three novels, *The Rebel Angels*, *What's Bred in the Bone*, and *The Lyre of Orpheus*.

His career has been marked by many honours: he was the first Canadian to become an Honorary Member of the American Academy and Institute of Arts and Letters. He is a Companion of the Order of Canada and an Honorary Fellow of Balliol. He and his wife now divide their time between homes in Toronto, and in Caledon, Ontario.

ROBERTSON DAVIES

A Chat About Literacy

Writer: So we're going to talk about literacy, are we? What do you think the word means?

Student: Being able to read and write; isn't that it?

Writer: That's it, certainly. But literacy is one of those words that means different things to different people. For instance, if I say that somebody is illiterate, what do you think I mean?

Student: That they can't read and write. Or not very much.

Writer: There, you see? Already you have made a qualification when you say, "not very much." There are hundreds of thousands of people who would be very cross if you called them illiterate, but it is true that they can't read and write very much. People who can't read and write at all are not numerous in a country like Canada. Most people can write their names, and they know what signs that say STOP and GO mean, and perhaps even

DANGER. But they can't read the directions on a bottle of medicine, for instance, or the handbook that comes with the car they are driving. Often they are clever at concealing the fact that the world of print is closed to them. That is a very dangerous kind of illiteracy.

Student: How many kinds of literacy do you suppose there are?

Writer: Suppose we say three. There is the kind we have just been talking about – being shut off from everything that requires understanding of even quite simple things that are written down. Of course that really only applies in a country like ours, where the written word is so important. There were millions of people in the past, and there are millions now, who do not live in what we might call the Verbal World. A hundred and fifty years ago you could be an efficient farmer or blacksmith without being able to read or write. You were a valuable person and you knew your job thoroughly. You could get somebody else to do any reading or writing you needed. But now we live in a world where that is impossible. Though there are other parts of the world – Central Africa, for instance – where reading and writing count for very little – it would be wrong to say that people who do not belong to our Verbal World are stupid. Millions of those people want to join the Verbal World, and CODE helps them. But we are talking about our world, right here, which is very much part of the Verbal World.

Student: But you said there were three kinds of literacy. What is Number Two?

Writer: Number Two takes in all the people who can read and write, have no trouble with medicine bottles or books of directions, and may be skilled in technical work of some complexity. They read the newspapers; sometimes they read magazines. They don't pay much attention to books, unless the books are concerned with their work. Some of them are professional people who read and understand complicated books about law, and medicine, and insurance, and all kinds of business. They have fair-sized vocabularies and their grammar is pretty good, but not precise. No doubt about it, they are literate, in the Number Two sense of the word.

Student: What's Number Three, then? It seems to me you have been talking about everybody that matters.

Writer: The whole idea of literacy is filled with shady areas that overlap. The Number Two people can read anything that concerns them. But consider yourself, as an example. Do you want to join the adult world knowing your job and the daily news, and nothing else?

Student: I'm not sure I understand. What else is there?

Writer: What you have just asked me is the kind of question Socrates used to ask people when he wanted to make them think. I am sure you know what else there is that is involved in literacy. Do you know who Socrates was?

Student: Vaguely. He was a Greek philosopher, wasn't he?

Writer: Yes, and like you he pretended not to understand what people said in order to make them clarify their thinking. To a tremendous extent thinking is a matter of language.

Student: Yes, but everybody has language. Even the Number One people you talked about have language.

Writer: Not to the same degree that the Number Two people have language. And the Number Three people have language in a degree that the Number Ones and the Number Twos do not have it, because they can use it to extend their personal knowledge in a way that goes far beyond the others. They can use language to ask hard questions, and explore kinds of thinking that the Number Ones and the Number Twos never bother their heads about. They can define things accurately and they can discuss things intelligently about which strict accuracy is impossible. They are the people who enlarge human knowledge – perhaps only their own knowledge, or perhaps the knowledge of the whole world.

Student: Give me an example.

Writer: There you are, being Socratic again. Well – here's an example. Suppose you become a doctor, a healer. Are you going to be content with what you have learned in medical school, and never venture beyond it? I hope not. I hope you would be one of those who perpetually question what you have learned and look for new approaches to medicine. If nobody had ever done that we would still be treating tuberculosis by hanging bags of herbs around the necks of sick people, because that was what our teacher had told us.

Student: But that's thinking. What has that got to do with literacy? When I think of literacy I think about having to read books I am told to read in school – books that tell stories, or poems that don't even do that. I don't see how that teaches you to think.

Writer: Yes you do. Those books have taught you to think: What good is all this stuff? What does it tell me? That's thinking.

Student: In my class we have to read *Huckleberry Finn*. It's a pretty good book, but what does it teach me? What is there in *Huckleberry Finn* that is any good to me?

Writer: It teaches you a lot about the value of independent thought. Huck was a simple boy – a Number One, in fact, but an unusual Number One because he thought that slavery was wrong, and that black people have rights just as much as white people. That wasn't the kind of thinking he met with among the people around him, and he supposed he was a very wicked boy because he thought differently. But do you think he was wicked?

Student: Oh no. He was right. Everybody knows that. I

mean, anybody can see that slavery is wrong. Imagine owning somebody else, and buying and selling another person just as you pleased.

Writer: Not everybody knew that was wrong in Huck's time and a lot of people don't know it now. But you know it, and at least, in part, you have learned it from *Huckleberry Finn*. You are standing on Huck's shoulders, so you can see farther and clearer than he did. Now, about poetry –

Student: I don't see the use of poetry at all. Just a tangle of words.

Writer: Wait a minute. When I was about your age I had to memorize a poem that didn't mean much to me. It went like this:

> It is not growing like a tree
> In bulk, doth make Man better be;
> Or standing long an oak, three hundred year,
> To fall a log at last, dry, bald and sere:
> A lily of a day
> Is fairer far in May,
> Although it fall and die that night
> It was the plant and flower of light:
> In small proportions we just beauty see;
> And in short measure life may perfect be.

You see, I have remembered that for more than 60 years, and what it says – *That it isn't how long you live but how well you live* – is extremely important, and it has taken me a lifetime to understand all the poet meant.

Student: But why not say it just the way you said it? Why all the words?

Writer: Because my version lacks the splendour and beauty of the poem. And without splendour and beauty, what is the good of life?

Student: I don't get it?

Writer: But you will. The questions you have been asking tell me that you will. And that's what the Third Degree of literacy means. Splendour and beauty are the things that have lifted mankind out of the mud. And you don't want to stay in the mud.

Brian Doyle

Brian Doyle's great-grandfather came to Ottawa on a famine ship in 1847, and the Doyle family has resided there ever since. Born in 1935, Brian Doyle is the reading and writing teacher at Ottawa Technical High School. His books include *Hey Dad*, *You Can Pick Me Up at Peggy's Cove*, *Angel Square*, *Up to Low*, and *Easy Avenue*. The last two were both Canadian Library Association Books of the Year.

BRIAN DOYLE

from *Angel Square*

School wasn't getting along with me very well lately. And I wasn't getting along very well with it.

It pretty well started back when I was in grade five and Miss Strong just laughed at me when I said I wanted to be a writer when I grew up.

She didn't really laugh, I guess, she just made a kind of sound with her mouth like you would if you were blowing a little feather or a hunk of fluff off your upper lip just under your nose.

Or maybe it was way back in grade four when we had the I.Q. test. They gave all the grade fours an I.Q. test and I was the only one who had to go back the next day and do it over again. I saw Miss Frack and Miss Eck discussing mine. They were standing facing each other talking about my test. I knew because they looked over at me a couple of times. They both had huge chests and they were standing kind of apart so their chests wouldn't bounce off each other.

They looked like two huge robins discussing a worm.

There was a lot of sighing and then they came and told me that I'd have to do the test again the next day. By the looks on their faces I figured they were saying that they knew I was stupid, sure, but could I possibly be that stupid? Could I be something subhuman? You'd have to be in a coma or something to score that low.

But Dad said that maybe I scored so high that the test couldn't record it – maybe I blew out all the tubes in the thing and they figured only a genius could score that high and they figured something went wrong with their test because even Albert Einstein couldn't score that high.

And they say he invented the atomic bomb.

That made me feel a bit better.

But I didn't really blame Miss Strong for laughing when I said I wanted to be a writer.

After all, I was the second worst writer in the class.

Melody Bleach was the worst writer in the class. Her main problem was she never had a pencil and she couldn't write with a pen and a nib because she pressed too hard.

Dad said the reason was, she wasn't organized.

And she always put her tongue out when she tried to write after she borrowed a pencil or the teacher gave her one.

She'd stick her tongue between her teeth when she was trying to think of what to write. Some of the kids would laugh at her and make fun of her.

I laughed at her too but I also felt sort of sorry for her.

Specially when she wet herself. That was in grade three, I think. Melody wet herself. She was too scared of Miss

Frack or Miss Eck, or whoever it was, to ask if she could leave the room.

So she just sat there and the water ran down off the seat into a pool on the floor under her desk. And the water ran down her cheeks from her eyes. There was water running out of her from both ends.

I think Dad was right. Her main problem was that she wasn't organized. Dad always says, get organized and you can't go wrong.

Suddenly I heard Blue Cheeks saying my name. Everybody was looking over at me. And Blue Cheeks was getting bluer. He was asking me about a grammar sentence. He was writing on the blackboard but he was looking at me.

Blue Cheeks could turn his head *right* around without moving his body. His head would start turning slowly and it would keep turning and turning until it was facing the other way. Then it would start back until it was back almost to the same spot. He could turn his head left and right so far that he could cover the whole 360 degrees without moving his shoulders. His head must have been on a swivel or something.

He would write grammar sentences on the board so that we could copy them out and then tell him what was wrong with them.

All the sentences he ever wrote on the board were wrong.

Every day we wrote down hundreds of sentences that were wrong.

Some of them were quite funny but if he heard anybody

laughing or snorting, old Blue Cheeks's head would start coming around, slowly, slowly. And we'd all sit there, hypnotized by how far his head could come round.

I used to think it would unscrew and tumble right off onto the floor.

But then, of course, if that happened he could catch it just before it hit because his hands hung down there near the floor anyway.

Somebody must have coughed or something and he looked around and couldn't catch anybody so he noticed I was in a trance and picked me as his victim. I must have been staring into the blackboard like I was hypnotized. Dad said later that I must have looked like a cow watching a train go by.

"You! What is wrong with this sentence?"

He was pointing at the sentence he had just written on the board.

"Read the sentence, please," he said.

I read it. "Ralph edged closer as the moose sniffed suspiciously and snapped the picture," the sentence said.

"Well?" said Blue Cheeks.

I looked at the sentence again.

"Tell us, Mr. Daydreams, what is wrong with this sentence."

"It's something to do with the camera," I said.

"It's something to do with the camera, is it?" His head was right around facing me full-on now and his shoulders were still facing the blackboard. It seemed impossible.

"And the moose," I said, "and something to do with the moose."

"The camera and the moose," said Blue Cheeks, sarcasm dripping off his lips like syrup.

"And Ralph," I said, just to make sure, "there's something wrong with Ralph too."

"And what do you suppose it is that is wrong with Ralph?" said Blue Cheeks.

"He hasn't got the camera," I said.

"And who has the camera?"

"The moose seems to have the camera."

"And why has the moose got the camera instead of Ralph?"

"I don't know, sir. It seems strange, a moose with a camera."

"Why has the moose got the camera?"

"Maybe he took it from Ralph?"

"Why hasn't Ralph got his own camera?" Blue Cheeks's face was dark blue now.

"Maybe it *isn't* Ralph's camera!" I said, thinking I was on to something. "Maybe Ralph hasn't got a camera and the moose has a camera and Ralph's sneaking up on the moose to steal his camera!"

"Read the sentence again!"

"Ralph edged closer as the moose sniffed suspiciously and snapped the picture." I almost knew it off by heart now.

"What is wrong with that sentence?"

Behind me sat Geranium Mayburger, the dumbest girl in the school. Geranium loved to whisper answers to people. Specially people in trouble.

"Hooves," she whispered behind me. "A moose can't take a picture because his hooves are too big for the button."

"Five seconds," said Blue Cheeks, "or you stay and write lines!" He sounded like he was choking. I was desperate.

"A moose could never hold a camera properly or snap a picture because of its large and clumsy hooves," I said, trying to make the best sentence I could.

I knew I was doomed, so I sat down.

Blue Cheeks gurgled, "One hundred lines – 'I must learn my grammar'!"

A few minutes later the bell rang for recess and I was suddenly alone.

Excerpted from *Angel Square* (Groundwood Books, 1984), in slightly revised form. Reprinted by permission.

Joan Finnigan

Joan Finnigan was born and raised in Ottawa. She began full-time writing in 1965, following the death of her husband, Dr. Charles Grant Mackenzie. During this twenty-five-year period, she has produced many works for the CBC and the National Film Board, as well as publishing twenty-one books of poetry, plays, history, children's literature, and oral history. She has three children: Jonathan, Roderick, and Martha.

JOAN FINNIGAN

Print Your Name Large

I loved school! They say girls always do more than boys. I am sure I did more than all girls. Half a century later I still remember every detail of my kindergarten class at Percy Street School in Ottawa and, as for grade one where I learned to read, I can still see in my mind's eye and repeat for you the phonetic cards that lined the top of the blackboard on two sides of the room. I remember one time in that year being away from school ill and returning to find that the class had moved on to a new reader with these strange words like "cake" and "late" which made no sense at all when I sounded them out. In a state of panic I turned to a girl in the next row, a "repeater." "What are these words?" I gasped out to her, pointing to the phonetic rule-breakers. "The E makes the A say its own name," she whispered back to me. Oh magic, it worked! Nothing had been taken away from me. I was a very important person once again, a very important person once more on the road to fulfilling my thirst for learning, to realizing my potential.

In my past twelve years of taping the old-timers of Ottawa Valley, I have met a goodly number who, in the process of giving me their life story, have said to me, "Oh, if I'd only gone to school!" Or, "If I'd only got more schooling my life would have been different!" I have met some who opened one of my proffered books so hesitantly that I knew intuitively they could not read. I have talked with others who simply said, "I can only read the pictures." Yes, a goodly number of times I was faced with what I consider to be the ultimate tragedy and the greater immorality – human potential unfulfilled.

But a number of years ago in my work with the NFB I was involved in making a film on one of the precedent-setting rural classes for illiterates sponsored by the Ontario Government. "If you get to the main road, we'll pick you up," the flyer said. And so, in the depths of January, from all age groups and all racial origins, through the snows on foot or sometimes behind the jingling sleigh-bells of horse-drawn cutters, the people who burned to learn to read and write got to the main road and were picked up for the Adult Learning Courses at Combermere. And there the feisty little teaching-nun, inspired by the intensity of the motivation of her pupils, took as her refrain a line which has been etched on my brain ever since: "*You are a very important person. Print your name large.*"

Yes, how many older people, bright, curious, intelligent, even brilliant, have I known in my oral history work, even in my own network of Valley clans, whose lack of education not only limited their development of potential but who were also keenly aware of the deprivation and the loss? And how many have I known who perhaps have learned the fundamentals of reading and writing but whose love of reading was not sufficiently kindled in their younger years to enrich their later years, who now sit, hands folded, by kitchen windows or lie, bored and hopeless on institutional beds, unable to make the myriad magical journeys of the imagination which reading makes possible?

Believe me, I never negate the experiential learning and wisdom of the primitive tribes, Native Peoples, those who still live and work in the oral traditions. They have all kinds of riches of their own: the ability to live co-operatively; to do their own problem-solving often on the spot; to improvise and innovate for survival. These people took care of the earth – and still take care of the earth – far more than we of the so-called "civilized" and "educated" tribes of the Western World whose waste and greed, paradoxically, is bringing the whole earth to the brink of disaster. Throughout "The Global Village" the top priority today is the preservation of our environment and the solving of our ecological problems. All other issues pale beside such dire goals.

But, in a convoluted manner, learning to read is part of our preservation of the planet. For learning to read gives the individual his understanding of the Power of One, the Power of One to examine ideas, to ask questions, to demand political freedom, to exercise a vote, to claim individual rights to things like birth control, justice before the law, clean air. The Power of One developed by reading helps one to understand and believe in the power to change things. As the feisty little teaching-nun said in Combermere: "*You are a very important person! Print your name large.*"

Perhaps our sacrilegious North American waste of trees, pulp and paper can be counter-balanced by CODE's shipments of books and textbooks to Third World countries where all people, learning to read and write, will be given the Power of One to reject political confinements on freedom, to demand their human dignity, yes, perhaps even to find the strength to cry "No! Stop!" when their environment is about to be pillaged and polluted.

In our "Global Village" the Power of One can effect change. Learning to read fills one with a sense of the Power of One. It is the people who believe in the Power of One who effect change. Everywhere let the E make the A say its own name.

DONALD WINKLER

Sheila Fischman is one of Canada's foremost translators. Among the many French-Canadian writers she has translated into English are Roch Carrier, Michel Tremblay, Marie-Claire Blais, Anne Hébert, Jacques Poulin, and Yves Beauchemin. Her translation of Michel Tremblay's *Thérèse and Pierrette and the Little Hanging Angel* won the Canada Council Translation Prize in 1984. In 1989, she became the first winner of the Félix-Antoine Savard Prize offered by Columbia University.

SHEILA FISCHMAN

Our Friends

I remember the day when I learned to read. It was in December and there was a lot of snow on the ground. Earlier, my mother had bundled me into my good snow-suit, the royal blue one that had a coat nipped in at the waist and a sunbonnet-shape hat, and leggings with zippers at the ankles. It was Sunday, so the teenaged girl who lived across the street was not in school. She had sat me on my sleigh that afternoon and pulled me through the streets of our village, over thickly packed snow, as the thin winter light grew paler. Some months earlier a baby sister had been born, and I was entitled to certain privileges.

Back home from my sleigh-ride, I don't remember suffering that day from the usual cold hands, wet feet or dripping nose. What I do remember is going at once to a footstool next to the radio cabinet in a corner of the living-room, and hunching over a book with a royal-blue cover. This was a favourite posture of mine, for I loved to play at "reading." My parents must have encouraged my game, because I knew the alphabet. I still remember the frustration I would feel as I peered at the type on the pages. Some patterns of letters were recognizable, but mostly I felt I was looking at a puzzle to which the key had yet to be identified. (Later, I would experience this sensation again when I was learning to comprehend and speak French.) I wish I understood the combined activities of brain and eye that occurred; I only know that all at once the letters were no longer simply patterns, they were words. I said some of them aloud and heard someone exclaim, "She's reading!"

If this were a conventional and proper memoir, the book I was holding on that December afternoon just after my fourth birthday would be a classic of children's literature, an old storybook that had informed and entertained generations before me. But ours was not a literary family, not even a conventional well-educated one. My parents read two daily papers and *Maclean's* magazine, but until I started school there were few books in our house. Bedtime stories were told, not read. And so that first book in which I was able to pick out and string together words – the book from which I learned to read – was a schoolbook, a "reader," probably a stray from my parents' store.

It was a village general store, which abutted our house, where one "could buy anything from a paper of pins to diamond rings" as my parents proudly declared. In years to come what I loved most, though, as much as the glass jars of candy or the ice-cream dipped up with a heavy chrome scoop that is now mine, was the August day when the books arrived.

These were elementary and high school textbooks, and helping to unpack and arrange them in the back-to-school display was the only childhood task I didn't hate. The heavy cardboard cartons would be piled in a dusty storeroom lit weakly from the ceiling by two bare bulbs, and from one side by windows gray with a century of dust. My father would open his black-handled pocket-knife and slit the tape that sealed the boxes, then strip back the flaps and end-pieces, releasing the smell, sweet and dusty and crisp as apples, of new books.

Soon, books were added to the toys and dolls that had been my earliest companions. I was a shy and timid child, with a good memory but with little gift for invention. For years, my love of reading saved me from loneliness, though I know now that this precocious addiction did little to help make me a social creature.

Then as now, however, it was books, the written word, that represented and presented the world to me, more intimately and durably than any other medium. Of course they showed me other people, and distant places and times, but almost more important, they introduced me to people like myself, to young girls I thought I recognized, whose invented existence made me feel less strange. They accompanied me through the ordeal of adolescence, and helped me become sociable, even gregarious. Books prepared me to go into the world.

The world I eventually chose, after some years of groping through a variety of academic subjects and a job or two, was one dominated by books. I've sold them, reviewed them, promoted them to the press and public, and now I translate them from French into English. Books are the most important objects in my life. The first furniture I owned consisted of two planks and a small pile of bricks (faced with turquoise, for some reason) to hold my few paperbacks. My first purchase with my first paycheque was a book. In new cities, I head for the bookstores. And when books come to the house it's still exciting: sometimes because they contain my own work, but always because of the feel and the smell and the fresh crackling sound that a new book makes when it's opened.

I couldn't name a book that changed my life. Every one that I've read or skimmed or even glanced at has shaped me in some way. When a violent storm flooded our house a few years ago, threatening everything inside and its very foundations, my first act was to move to safety as many books as possible. I almost wept when some, unsalvageable, had to be discarded. When it was calm again and we were safe and dry, with most of the books back where they belonged, the man I share the house with – who courted me with books – extended his arms towards the crowded shelves and said, relieved, "Our friends."

JOHN EVANS

Tony German is an established author, a screenwriter, an experienced naval officer, and a businessman. His long and varied experience in government and the private sector includes naval operations and staff work in war and peace, running his own technical development business, parliamentary committee administration, education, training and youth programs, and the definition, research, and writing of documentary films. His historical novels for young adults are: *Tom Penny*, *River Race*, *Tom Penny and the Grand Canal*, and *A Breed Apart*.

Tony German was born in Ottawa in 1924. He lives on Kingsmere Lake in the Gatineau with his wife, Sage, and their large white poodle, Chickadee. His latest book, *The Sea Is at Our Gate: the History of the Canadian Navy*, will be published in the spring of 1990.

TONY GERMAN

What Book Are You Taking?

"What book are you taking?" I said to my small son. We were crouched on the kitchen floor, the two of us, stuffing our packs on the eve of his first canoe trip.

He said, "I've got no room." I'd just told him that everything we took had to be packed across the portages, and underlined the lesson by barring his new football.

"Never be without a book," I said. Even in 1957 no such opportunity should be missed. "There's no TV. And if we get pinned down by a storm we can stay in the tent and read. A book's your best friend, you know."

He looked at me sideways. That last was a little too much and it was old stuff except for the twist about the storm. He didn't speak.

"How about one book between us, then?" I ventured.

"Okay," he said, still miffed about the football. "*You* choose and put it in *your* pack."

What book are you taking? In my own childhood, when packing for the holidays, "book" was always singular. You might squeeze two small ones into your suitcase at a pinch but selection was rather more critical in those far-off times; you couldn't cover slipshod choice with a handful of paperbacks. So which would it be? *Treasure Island*? You'd just finished it the third time. The new Tom Swift wouldn't last. You cantered through his latest in electric cars and submarines and airships in no time. That hefty birthday volume from Auntie Vi? *Lorna Doone*, all 646 pages, with 16 colour illustrations?

The girl's name for a title made it suspect, but a flip-through had revealed that "I" was a spirited young fellow who grew to a sturdy giant of a yeoman, and the pictures smacked well enough of adventure and daring deeds. The sheer bulk of it was a little daunting but there'd be more than enough time, what with the train trip and rainy days and of course at night in bed when it was absolutely mandatory to read under the covers by flashlight long past the last firm "lights out" shouted up the stairs. And the chapters were snappy – 75 of them, less than ten pages each.

So, for our canoe-trip choice, I took those memories to our shelf of childhood books, my wife's mostly, a precious trove that had moved with us for years. They ranged from a huge dog-eared *Mother Goose* to *The Secret Garden*, *The Water-Babies*, all the Christopher Robins, and *Peter Pan*; *Alice*, with Tenniel's drawings; *Just-So Stories*, and *Kim*; *The Romance of King Arthur* – Malory's richly convoluted medieval style abridged enough and leavened enticingly with Arthur Rackham's magic illustrations. Even Baroness Orczy's thriller about the Scarlet Pimpernel was there, and Rider Haggard's *King Solomon's Mines*, and *She*. There was my old *Treasure Island* too, *Robin Hood* and, of course, *Lorna Doone* – which had in fact proved not to be my taste. I picked *The Wind in the Willows*.

My son was still a little guy so this wasn't a very long canoe trip and not too far afield. But wherever it is, when you're in your canoe and away and across that first portage, what's real is here and now. The rest of the world is left, utterly irrelevant and far behind. So we paddled and portaged and pitched our tent and assembled stones for a fireplace and split a cedar stump for wood. We scorched our strips of first-night-out steak and pronounced them the finest ever. The sky's red luminescence doubled in the glassy lake and the light began to fade. At the thrum of the first nighthawk he'd ever heard he jumped clear out of his skin, and we crawled, secure, into our sleeping bags.

Now the final, the most marvellous pleasure of the day. The tent flaps are back. Over your toes, through the mosquito net are the embers of the fire and the pine against the sky, the lake a slowly darkening mirror. Then the match, the soft glow of the candle, and from my pack the book, and I begin to read. The words weave their spell on both of us, close together as we are. A loon calls, eerie, lonely from far across the lake, and the small boy edges just a trifle closer – he says so he can see the pictures better.

The Wind in the Willows. Badger and Toad, the recalcitrant motor-car, the Water Rat rowing Mole up the gentle river. And nothing, as Rattie says, ". . . absolutely nothing like simply messing about . . . in boats. . . ."

The loon's call on our lake is nearer now, and with a different note. I read on, entranced. The gentle light dissolves the canvas of our tent and we're there on Rattie's river. But the loon's cry is now quite close, and it's changed again. Changed to laughter: raucous, mocking – yes, mocking laughter. He's heard me, that loon says; he's heard the tale I'm reading to my son. And on this lake in this timeless, harsh-hewn land I'm reading of some water rat rowing some mole up some bland, English, meadow-bordered stream. What, pray tell, is this?

I can only plead, tell him, "Loon, my bookshelf brims with enchantment. Yes, it's from elsewhere, but it's enchantment none the less." That's not enough for him. "Tell us," he taunts, "tell him, tell me, tell us – about ourselves." His voice fades till it's just a scornful echo. The candle is very low. Its small flame lights my son's face, fast asleep, and there's a catch in my throat as I blow it out.

Last summer I took my grandson on his first canoe trip, just the two of us again, and along the self-same route. Thirty-two years, surprisingly, had changed it not that much. Some more cottages on the first lake and, spanning the outlet stream, a small bridge. But the water still riffled there just enough for a youngster to call it a rapid and catch his breath. We stopped for our afternoon swim on the deserted island grown with balsams where we had stopped before. I showed him the old game of puncturing the blistered bark with a twig for a glob of amber gum, then putting it in the water and seeing the gummy end exude the irridescent film that magically propelled the twig ahead. Balsam boats placed side by side made a fine unpredictable race.

At the portage there was regretful change: a road in, and the inevitability of cottages to come. The old canoe bore harder on the shoulders and I had to make a second trip for my pack. But paddling on we found our campsite, lovely as ever and not a soul in view. Tent, fire, steak over the coals, and cindered, gooey marshmallows for dessert. Then, snug in our sleeping bags, I asked, "What book did you bring?"

"Dad told me you'd bring the book," he said.

I had of course. I'd been waiting for this for a very long time. The book – written years after the loon had challenged me to do so in this very place – began, not on Mole's and Rattie's sun-splashed backwater, but far up the mighty Missinippe with a blazing fire catching trail-hardened faces, and the growl of the Shagenaw rapid in your ears. It was too – and I believe this to be fair – more digestible than *Lorna Doone*. It was certainly more compact. I read on with deep joy and with growing humility. The back of my mind, from my youngest days had been so richly filled with the works of those great creators of our childhood books that it simply had to burst out in some imaginings wrapped around experience of my own.

The debt lay with them; my loon had been the trigger. But he didn't call while I was reading, as I'd hoped so hard that he, or at least a grandchild to whom he'd handed on the tale, would do. The march of civilization, I told myself, isn't kind to loons. And now the boy was fast asleep.

We did hear him though, very early in the morning. He woke us both and we took a misty paddle round the bay with the fishing rod, casting off the lily-pads for our breakfast. The call went on, though we never saw him, and it had in it a note of exaltation that was very close to what was in my heart.

BRIAN A. KILGORE

Peter Gzowski, born in Toronto, raised in what he still calls Galt, Ontario (more formally, it's now Cambridge), has been the host of CBC Radio's "Morningside" since 1982. He has won seven ACTRA awards and, in 1989, was presented with the John Drainie award for his contributions to Canadian broadcasting. At points in his checkered career, he has been editor of *Maclean's* magazine and the *Star Weekly*, a newspaper columnist, and the author of scores of magazine articles. (He has also won three National Magazine Awards.) He has published ten books, as writer or editor, including three best-selling anthologies of letters to "Morningside." His books include *Spring Tonic*, *The Sacrament*, *The Game of Our Lives*, *This Country in the Morning*, *An Unbroken Line*, *The Morningside Papers*, and *The Private Voice*. Peter Gzowski's golf tournaments for literacy, whose origins he describes in this anthology, now number six, and reach from Victoria to Fredericton.

PETER GZOWSKI

Beyond Statistics

The game of golf has had so much to do with my own involvement with literacy that, if I don't pause to think about it, the story I want to tell here, which involves a golf *pro* and how she got caught up too, seems almost inevitable, as if there could have been no other conclusion. I tell it, though, for what it shows about what both she and I now call simply "the cause," and with the hope that others will think about its point, and maybe even want to join in.

My involvement, as I've written elsewhere, began casually and serendipitously. In the summer of 1985, I was feeling very lucky about things. A couple of years earlier, after a long and miserable time away, I had returned to CBC Radio. To my intense relief, I had found myself able to pick up where I had left off, and the program I was hosting, *Morningside*, was going better than I might have dared to hope. By 1985 – *Morningside* affords its host a much-needed summer hiatus – I had found a cottage in the part of Ontario where my grandparents had summered when I was a child, and had taken up once again, and on the same course I had played with my grandfather, the game of my youth. Playing golf one day with the woman who shares both that cottage and my life (I can still remember where the idea was born, as I contemplated a challenging six-iron into the eighth green and revelled in the summer air and the sound of birds), I began to wonder about holding a tournament for my friends. If I did it right, I might even raise a little money. It would, I thought, give me both a chance to say thank you for my good fortune and, perhaps, an excuse to turn down some of the too-many other functions, all for good causes, I was constantly invited to attend.

Only then – how strange it seems to write this now, when the literacy movement fills every spare corner of my life – did I begin to think about what to raise the money *for.*

My mind went back to the previous radio season. I had interviewed a woman who had grown up in the Palestinian refugee camps and come to Canada as a teenager. She was smart enough to bluff her way around her inability to decipher letters. Among the jobs she'd held before she came out of the closet and took reading lessons (she has an MA now) was a spell in the McGill University library, a feat she brought off by memorizing the size and colour of the books on the shelves. Her story, which made a profound impression me, had disabused me forever of the notion that illiteracy implied a lack of intelligence, and, inspired by her accomplishments, I had begun to sniff around the edges of the Canadian situation. Literacy, as a cause, was still not fashionable here; the figures Peter Calamai (who played in my first tournament) later turned up for the Southam newspaper chain were not yet available. But, as with many still-unfashionable concerns, there were a lot of dedicated people working out of the limelight.

One of them, I remembered, had been nagging me by mail. He was John O'Leary of Frontier College, who had heard my interview with the refugee and detected my own interest. In his letters, he had suggested I recruit what he called "The *Morningside* Army" to help the college in its then-pioneering work of teaching reading. Since books and writing were (and are) a seminal part of my life (I'm a librarian's kid as well as a struggling author), he had struck a chord. But I was unwilling to use the public facilities of the CBC as a medium of advocacy for even so uncontroversial a cause. A game of golf on my own time, though, was different. I called John and asked him if he thought a tournament to raise both money and some public awareness would be an acceptable idea, and by the next spring we were off and running.

Now, not quite five years after the idea dawned, the informal tournament I wanted to hold for a few friends, has become almost a national chain: the Peter Gzowski Invitationals. We've had four at the Briars, my grandfather's old course, two in Ottawa, one on Vancouver Island. As I write this – fresh from our debut in Victoria, where we made $18,000, and after which the mayor of Vancouver, who had flown across the Gulf of Georgia to join us, expressed an interest in holding one in *his* city – we have firm plans for Calgary (1990), and at least sketchy ones for Saskatchewan, Prince Edward Island and . . . who knows?

We've raised something over $300,000 so far, and the pledge I scribble recklessly on a cocktail napkin after our first heady event at the Briars – a napkin that might have been a little damp with Scotch whisky, I admit, on which I wrote that I would raise a million dollars before I was through – now seems possible to fulfil. As well – and I could not have known how important these other aspects would be when we began – our tournaments (now supported by national sponsors that range from Air Canada to Labatt's, and from the Post Office to Petro-Can, and featuring music, poetry, a mixture of golfers that has extended from George Knudson and Sandra Post to rank beginners, and in which we've managed to mix a lot of powerful people from business and the professions with a lot of workers for literacy) have helped recruit both attention and new people to the cause, not to mention having turned me, from my almost incidental initiation, into a fervent missionary. The more tournaments I've held, the more I've learned about the reason I hold them; the more I've learned, the more I've wanted to help.

Which brings me, at last, to my golf pro.

Her name is Danielle Nadon. She's in her early thirties, fluently bilingual (and, I hasten to add, comfortably literate not only in English and French but in the Spanish she's acquired on the international golf tour), the mother of a ten-year-old. A natural athlete, she picked up golf at university and turned professional shortly after graduation. She was a student of George Knudson's and shares not only George's fluid swing and ability to teach but his insouciance about putting. Like Knudson, she loves to hit the ball, she plays with joy. Once, on a friendly round with her, I watched her follow the missing of an eight-foot birdie putt with a booming, 240-yard drive. I asked her whether she'd rather have made the putt or hit the drive – about thirty yards past my own quite impressive (I'd thought) best effort. "Are you *kidding*?" she said. "A high handicapper might have made that putt. But you have to really swing to hit a drive like that." She is, in other words, a creature of enthusiasms.

I met her our first year in Ottawa, where she was the pro at our host club. She played a round with us, and enjoyed herself and the tournament so much that the next year she came – at her own expense – to the Briars, which is where, I think it's fair to say, she got hooked.

It was our poet who did it. Poets, as I've indicated, have been a part of all the Invitationals. From the beginning, we wanted to underline the literary aspects of why we were playing golf by commissioning a poet laureate for each tournament. He (or she) would simply spend the day with us, and, at the concluding ceremonies, offer the players a poem about what had occurred, just as the bards of old used to sing the occasions of their time. The idea had worked beyond our wildest imagining. In the first three years at the Briars, for example, Dennis Lee, Michael Ondaatje, and (bless her memory) Bronwen Wallace, all established stars, had given us spontaneous compositions that drew a standing ovation from the golfers whose achievements they celebrated – or, in passing, gently mocked.

For the fourth tournament the year Danielle came down from Ottawa, we wanted to ring a change. With the co-operation of people from Frontier College, I invited a writer not even the most studious of our golfers could have heard of, since she had never been published. Her name was Carole Boudrias. She's a single mother of five who, after a childhood and adolescence strewn with violence and poverty, had, with great courage, determined to learn to read and write. For the purposes of the tournament, the punchline of her story was that money we had raised by playing golf had made that possible for her, so, as you can imagine, the moment when she read her poem, seven deceptively simple stanzas that packed a wallop of both humour and grit, was one of high emotion – as well as being, I confess unabashedly, a handy inspiration to solicit even more financial support from our patrons.

What lingered in Danielle's mind, though, was an insight she had gained privately the evening before. At the pre-tournament barbecue, the golf pro and the learner, both mothers and sharing a first language, found themselves chatting quietly in a corner. Afterward – and I can still see Danielle shaking her head in wonder – she came up to me in another corner and said, simply, "You know, if you can't read, you can't cook."

That's true, you know. Oh, you can muddle through, imitating your mother or asking other people what they're doing – just as, for example, you can work in a library if you can memorize books by size and colour. But it's hard. You can't read recipes (just as you can't understand the menu in a restaurant), can't make out the directions on the packages, can't, if there are no pictures, even know what's in the cans. The woman who accepted a symbolic cheque for the money we raised in Victoria, for example, another amazing single mother who had raised four children before she went back to school said, in a brief speech that brought the golfers to their feet even *before* Susan Musgrave read her poem, "I don't know how I did it."

And, hearing what not reading had meant to Carole Boudrias, Danielle Nadon, creature of enthusiasms, was moved as no statistic ever could have moved her.

Except for the friendly round we played at her new club – she's the general manager of historic Chaudière now, across the river from Ottawa – I didn't see Danielle after the 1989 Briars tournament until we went to Victoria in the fall. By then, she was as given over to the tournaments and their purpose as I was, a kind of pro in residence to the Gzowski Invitationals; she had joined the Ottawa committee and, by phone, was helping plan our now burgeoning expansion.

In Victoria, her golf was spectacular. I put her in a foursome with a local newspaperman, a serious golfer renowned for his public disdain for, in order, feminists and French-Canadians, and, her usually almost unaccented English growing more *habitant* with every hole, she took delight in beating him convincingly. The rest of the time, though, she spread the word about literacy, cornering the captains of local business and power with tales of what they could do, and how important the work was.

When the Victoria tournament was over, a group of us, Bill Ardell, the president of Coles bookstores (a supporter from the start), Kevin Peterson, publisher of the *Calgary Herald* and his wife Sheila O'Brien, head of public affairs for Petro-Can (Kevin and Sheila are the moving spirits for Calgary), Bob Duncan, a filmmaker from Montreal who has moved to Vancouver and wants to help take us there, and a few other veterans, gathered for a drink, exhilarated yet again by the good feelings of a day on the course. The talk ranged far and wide, and I'm not sure how we came around to it, but suddenly Danielle had the floor.

"I haven't told you about my brother-in-law, have I?" she was asking. "He's 58 I think, married to my husband's oldest sister. At one of our family gatherings over the summer, I was talking about the tournaments and what the money goes for . . . you know, just chatting, the way we all do. And afterward, he came up to me.

"'You were talking to me, weren't you?' he said.

"I said no, I hadn't been, but . . . Anyway, you know what? He's illiterate? I never realized that. When he told me, of course, I remembered all the clues I might have seen – the way when we went to a restaurant and the menus were passed around, he'd always say 'Oh, I'll just have the same as you,' or how, when you were reading a newspaper, he'd come up behind you and say, 'Anything interesting today?' All the signs – except, of course, I couldn't see them. Fifty-eight years old, and I never realized. . . ."

There was a silence for a while. And then, while Bill Ardell ordered another round of drinks, we began figuring out how, before we left Victoria, we could all get together for a round at the fabulous course at Royal Colwood. But before we could even arrange partners for that foursome – everyone wanted Danielle as a partner, I noticed – we started talking about a letter that had come across my desk the week before, from Saskatchewan. There was a literacy group in Prince Albert, working with the prisoners in the penitentiary there, and the author of the letter wondered if, if she could get us on the course at Waskesiu, we'd like to start a tournament there.

"I don't know about the rest of you," said Danielle Nadon. "But I'm in."

PATRICIA WILSON

Dorris Heffron was born in Quebec and raised in various places near Toronto. She has an Honours B.A. and an M.A. in Literature and Philosophy from Queen's University. She lived in Oxford, England from 1969 to 1980, where she was a Tutor for Oxford University and for The Open University. There she began writing novels about teenagers, which were regarded as pioneers in "Young Adult" fiction. She has published three novels, two of which have been put on high-school literature courses in Canada and Europe.

Dorris Heffron has served on the National Council of The Writers' Union, on the Executive of PEN Canada, and on the Board of Directors of Na-Me-Res. Currently writer-in-residence at Wainfleet Public Library, she is writing an adult novel with the working title *Not a Short Story*.

DORRIS HEFFRON

The Saving Note

How do you tell if someone is literate or not? I used to assume that everyone was, in Canada, if they spoke the language. That was an assumption I grew up with, growing up in Canada in the 50s and 60s. During the 70s I lived abroad. I remember feeling offended when I returned to Canada and heard it said at a public meeting that perhaps 20 per cent of the country is functionally illiterate.

"That can't be true!" I argued.

And was wrong again. It was something I was willing to assume about other countries but not about my own. However, one gets used to being wrong. Eventually I accepted the truth and went to work on it.

I became a member of the board of directors of the Native Men's Residence in Toronto. There we found highly intelligent and artistically talented native men who would cleverly get the secretary to read aloud to them any forms or documents which they were required to sign. They would then pretend to reread the document themselves, before they scrawled their signature. The secretary was often told what a nice voice she had. She was pleased and they got their reading done for them. Eventually, she caught on, informed us on the board and a literacy program was set up in the residence.

Of course, illiteracy is not confined to the cities or to our native people. I am currently writer in residence at a library in a small village where the heritage is mainly Anglo-Saxon and European. I'm working with the exceptionally literate, those who want to become writers, at the same time that a program is being set up for some people in this same community who cannot read.

I've had to realize that my assumptions about literacy in my country were mightily wrong. Of course, this is nothing new: the wrongness of my assumptions. But it did get me to thinking about the importance of literacy and how, one time, it saved my life. I was saved by a note.

It was not a very flattering note. It wasn't even telling the truth. But it was clever and courageous, even gallant on his part, on the part of him about whom I had made perhaps *outrageous* assumptions.

It happened back in the 60s, when I was a university student hitch-hiking around Europe for four months, on $400. I did this by living on bread and cheese, and hitching from youth hostel to youth hostel. Never alone. I had assured my mother that I would never be so foolish as to hitch-hike alone. Girls don't. That much we agreed on.

Things went well for the first couple of months. I saw Britain and Ireland with other students who were literally going my way. There were adventures, some very enriching, none perilous. Then I moved onto the continent, with a bicycle I had bought to cycle to Paris with a young Harvard student.

Paris proved too much for me, money-wise. And all those surly shopkeepers who sold me bread and cheese with never a smile! Canadians *assume* smiles. And I was a cheerleader Canadian.

I decided to hot-foot it down to Greece where I could live on a dollar a day, stop all this hitching around, and flop on the beach to read and write for a month or two.

I smiled widely as I sold my bike to a Parisian shopkeeper for more than I had paid for it in England. Then I made my way down to Barcelona where I could get a cheap boat trip to Genoa, avoiding the expensive French Riviera. I would hitch down through Italy to catch the cheap fare from Brindisi to Athens. It was on the boat to Genoa that I met the stranger who would show me the value of literacy.

I was surely right in assuming that he was no student. He was young but he looked sinister. He never smiled. He didn't talk to people. He leaned against the ship's rail, smoking, watching the sea, watching people. He watched me but did not approach. He was dressed all in black, from his black Spanish hat down to his black cowboy boots. He carried a black guitar case, seldom set it down, never opened it. One could assume it contained a gun or drugs.

The boat began to dock at Genoa. I was uneasy because there was no one apparent to hitch to the hostel with. The black-clothed stranger approached me, not smiling. He spoke in a language I couldn't understand. I smiled and shrugged my shoulders. He looked impatient. He said "Greece."

I said, "What?"

"*Greece*," he repeated, then set down his guitar case, got out a little black book, and wrote "Go to Greece?" pointing at me as he showed me the words.

"Yes." I nodded in surprise.

With me? he indicated in sign language, pointing his finger hard into his chest. Then he held up his thumb, indicating that our mode of travel would be hitch-hiking.

Was it more dangerous to hitch-hike alone, or with this guy?

I figured if he could get me to the youth hostel, I'd be safe enough once there.

"Youth hostel?" I said, and indicated by holding up my thumb that I'd hitch with him to the youth hostel.

He frowned, looked irritated, but nodded in agreement. I put my rucksack on my back. We set off from the docks together.

It was clear from the way he conversed with drivers who stopped to offer us a ride, that he spoke Italian. Three cars stopped and were sent on again by my partner. He indicated that they were not going our way.

"Hey," I said, becoming alarmed. "We can't pass up every one."

"Jacko," he said, pressing his finger hard into his chest. He was to be called Jacko, not Hey.

The next car he made me get into. At breakneck speed, on those wide, winding Italian motorways, it took us all the way to Florence. He seemed to know the city extraordinarily well.

"Youth hostel," I kept saying as we maneuvred our way further into the city by public transport. He kept silent until we stopped at a street which was picturesque as a postcard of Florence.

"Come," he said, and led me up steps into a house which turned out to be his. His little old mother, dressed in black, cried as she embraced her son. Then she welcomed me, fed us both a three-course meal and showed me to a tiny bedroom where I spent the next three nights. By day, Jacko showed me around Florence, which I still remember as one of the most beautifully interesting cities I have seen. Through written notes he explained to me that he had some business to do in Florence, then he would hitch with me to Brindisi where we would catch the boat to Greece. Each afternoon he went about his business, while I looked around Florence.

I was happy, intrigued, and very well looked after. The guitar case was opened. It did contain a guitar, but still I assumed it contained more. Else why did he carry it around Florence with him, and never stop to play it?

We left Florence one sunny, very bright morning. We had good rides until late afternoon. The driver was an Italian man who kept looking over his shoulder at me and saying things to Jacko which evidently angered Jacko. Jacko shouted. He told the driver to stop and let us out. He did so, and sped off, spinning dust into our faces.

We were on a lonely highway far up into the hill country where the only sound was of sheep bleating in the distance. The hills were reddish and sparsely treed. Jacko kicked the ground and cursed the driver who had let us out there. "Nazi Pig" was what I understood from Jack's curses.

The sun was beginning to set. This was *not* youth hostel country. We were in the middle of the Italian nowhere. Not a car in a sight. . . . It was beginning to get dark when a car, a small, very old black car, came down the road. Two men were in it. They stopped and talked to Jacko. Jacko shook his head in refusal when they opened the back door, inviting us to get in. They then shook their heads and drove on. Jacko told me through gestures and the few words which I could by now understand from him, that the men were peasants offering a ride only to their village nearby. We needed a ride all the way to Brindisi.

A half hour later, the same car came by again. This time it was full of men. Dark-eyed, leering, muscular, purposive peasants. Jacko stepped in front of me as one of them leaned out the passenger-side window and began what were clearly negotiatons with Jacko.

A perfectly rational fear suddenly seized me. Without understanding the language, I knew what the words were saying. They wanted Jacko to give me to them. There were five of them. They laughed and leered. One of them began to shout at Jacko. The back door opened and two short men got out. Short, but strong. Their fists were clenched. Muscles in their arms flexed.

Jacko was saying something to them which made them halt, then sneer, then laugh derisively and argue. Jacko turned and said two words to me which I couldn't understand. He repeated them. I simply could not understand either his language or his accent.

Was he saying yes to them? Would he let them take me in exchange for giving him a ride all the way to Brindisi? That's what they seemed to be offering. Would Jacko make that kind of deal with them? And what might they do to the both of us if he didn't?

I knew he was determined to get to Greece tomorrow. He had business to do there. Deals, I assumed. I had assumed almost from the start that he was probably carrying something illicit in that guitar case and that travelling with a girl made him less suspicious looking. It certainly helped him get rides! I tried to appeal to him with my eyes as he turned to me, but he looked down. He reached into his pocket and got out his little black book, in which he wrote and then showed to me two words.

"Look sick."

Look sick?

Right! At this point, anything! I held onto his arm and began to half-faint, which is not far from what I truly felt like doing.

The peasants stared at me. They talked amongst themselves. They got back into the car. They drove off, shouting things out the window which no doubt very articulately expressed their feelings about foreign women in general and me in particular.

Jacko picked up his knapsack, his guitar already in hand, and made me follow him, fast, up the hill and far out of sight into a grove of trees.

There we spent the night in our separate sleeping bags. Every so often I would see Jacko get up and look around. He kept watch all night. In the morning, we went back down to the highway and quite soon got a ride in a Mercedes, all the way to Brindisi.

I parted from Jacko at the youth hostel in Athens. There, through a translator, I learned how Jacko knew, way back in Barcelona, that I was on my way to Greece.

"All American girls go to Greece," he said through our translator. "It is a natural assumption."

And what had he said to the peasants which had so effectively persuaded them that they didn't want me, after all?

He told them I was ill, ill with a disease common to the loose habits of foreign women, that I was contaminated. The name of the disease he did not write down for me. He just smiled and laughed and shook my hand.

"*Ciao*," he said.

OLD MASTERS STUDIO LTD.

Jack Hodgins is the author of such award-winning books as *Spit Delaney's Island*, *The Invention of the World*, *The Resurrection of Joseph Bourne*, *The Barclay Family Theatre*, and *The Honorary Patron*. A Governor General's Award winner, he also received the Canada Australia Literature Prize, and has read from his work in countries as distant as Japan, Austria, and Australia. His most recent book, *Left Behind in Squabble Bay* (a children's book), was published in 1989.

Jack Hodgins and his family live in Victoria, B.C., where he teaches at the University of Victoria. He is completing his next novel.

JACK HODGINS

Leaving Home: A Memoir

1944. They hadn't even brought the war to an end and already my parents were giving me something else to worry about. It would soon be time for me to start school, they said. Of course I had no intention of going through with this. I knew immediately what they were up to. This was to be an expulsion. While my younger brother would be allowed to stay home, I was to be sent, every day, out of the family, out of the house, and right off the stump ranch altogether – sent off to take my chances with unpredictable authorities on foreign territory.

Of course they tried to fool me into thinking that this was something I wouldn't want to miss.

"You'll learn to read!"

I had an answer to that. "I already know how to read."

True and not quite true. I had discovered that if I climbed the hanging ladder up through the little square hole in the kitchen ceiling I would enter the cool, shadowed world of the attic, where owners before us had left behind a supply of newspaper weekend comics – the funny papers. Mutt and Jeff. The Katzenjammer Kids. By staring and staring for hours on end, I eventually figured out what the characters must be saying to one another in order to make sense of their actions. I had, as far as I was concerned, learned how to read.

"Don't be ridiculous," my mother said. "Those funnies are all in Finnish. The people before us had them sent from Finland. What good is that to you? In school they'll teach you how to read *English*."

Wasn't *speaking* English enough? Surely staring at those Finnish comics had taught me skills that would serve to unlock the secrets of books in *any* language!

My cousin Tricia sneered. She knew I was doomed, while she had another year of freedom. She had still not quite forgiven me for setting a match to her great Orphan Annie head of bright red ringlets. Well, I had got fed up with the way adults always made such a fuss over that fiery head of hair. Besides, I hadn't really expected more than the ends to burn. To my surprise, I discovered that adults will make every bit as much fuss over a little girl's singed scalp.

Now consider what they expected me to give up, in exchange for a schoolroom full of "new friends" and some books to read.

First, the sleeping veranda. Outside the kitchen door, past the cream separator, past the woodbox, past the long green wooden bench with the row of caulk boots and gumboots beneath it and the row of rubbery smelling raincoats and grease-smelling plaid mackinaws above it, past the thumping, foaming wringer washing-machine with the foot-pedal motor smelling of gasoline beneath it. Turn the corner and there – the length of the house – a row of our summer beds, toy boxes waiting beneath them, a huge bag of dressup clothes hanging on the wall, a ledge to peer over while shooting at the armies which advanced through the long grass of the orchard, knot-holes to pee through, cracks in the floor to whisper secret messages through to whatever dogs, chickens, or cousins had crawled beneath the house. Here was where I had encouraged my cousin Tricia in her first experiment in human flight off the veranda rail. The clumps of couch-grass and soft patch of mint below taught her a valuable lesson about the limitations of human life while hardly even messing up her spectacular head of hair. Why would I want to give this up for a desk with a view of nothing more exciting than a blackboard?

Or this. Between the house and the field which stretched down the slope to the willows and the shallow swamp, there was a narrow orchard, a barbed wire fence entangled with morning glories, and a gigantic rock pile. As long as the house, much higher than the fence, and at least as wide as the chicken shed, the rock pile continued to grow with the new stones heaved up each year mysteriously from beneath the surface of the field. A few of these were as small as my fist or my knee but some were as large as I was myself, or larger – great angular lumps with rust streaks and embedded glitter and large green whorls; huge pointed anvils, flat slabs, round meteors. Blackberry vines were a prickly net that seemed to hold the whole thing together. Garter snakes disappeared into the holes but could not be followed. Invisible frogs croaked out from deep inside. When you'd climbed to the top you could find thrones to sit on while you dictated orders, cliffs to push red-headed captured Indians over, and depressions to slip down into while you piloted this submarine through enemy waters. And you could always hope to stumble on an entrance to the inside. Of course there *was* no inside. Only its surfaces yielded to play; the interior could only be imagined.

The interiors of stumps, however, were sometimes entirely accessible – and here was something else I was expected to give up for the better part of every day. Loggers had gone through this valley at the end of the previous century, cutting down the virgin forest from springboards wedged into the trunks ten feet up in the air. Later, a forest fire had swept through, burning the new growth and charring the stumps left behind by the logging. Since then, alders and second-growth fir and poplars had grown high and thick, grass and salal and hardhack had sprung up where fields had not yet been cleared and harrowed and seeded and rock-picked and manured. But the logging and the forest fire between them had left us a thousand blackened stumps and charred logs to make the fenced-off cattle pastures far more interesting than either true field or forest could be – certainly more interesting than the cattle pastures of the picture books. These stumps were ten feet high and anywhere from six to 15 feet across. Many of them were hollow – centres had rotted out. They smelled of dirt and ashes, the memory of epic fire. You could run your hand down the shiny black checked and scaley wall and hear the voices of nineteenth-century loggers passing through, could hear the roar of the fire sweeping down out of the mountains driving animals and people before it, could hear the footsteps of Indians stalking deer. Those which could be entered through narrow doorway gaps were often large enough inside to become houses, mansions, castles, with furniture constructed from broken lumber and stones stolen from the rock pile. Those stumps which could be entered only from below, by crawling on bellies up narrow tunnels through the twisted network of dead roots, were perfect hideouts, meeting places, and headquarters for international spy rings. Those which could be entered only from the top, with the help of a ladder, were perfectly suited for the role of dungeon when unwanted cousins and pain-in-the-neck friends of neighbours forced themselves upon us and did not respond well to orders. The long black horizontal trees lying thick as ships across the ground with their snaky roots standing up at one end made ideal vessels for the escapades of pirates. Lookouts braced themselves in the crotches of the highest roots. Captains could pace the entire length of the log, swinging a sword and shouting down mutineers. From this giant ship deep in the labyrinthine pasture, cows could be picked off while they grazed on clumps of grass, stump-castles could be surprised and captured, and the barely visible roof of the neighbour's steam bath could be blasted to smithereens by a well-aimed shot from an imaginary cannon on the deck. On a Sunday afternoon, if enough relatives had stopped by, every stump on the far side of the barn could have its own inhabitants, every charred fallen tree its full complement of sailors. Newcomers were given spears of huckleberry branches and turned into guards, or soldiers. Those we had hoped not to see were left to flounder in the waters to drown, begging for permission to enter our hostile world. My cousin Tricia cackled merrily within her chosen stump, where she stirred a concoction of weeds and lizards in a giant pot and waited for the curious and unpopular to stumble into her range, where they would soon find themselves tied and preparing to participate in a cannibal stew.

In order to persuade me to give all this up in exchange for a desk, a few schoolmates, and a teacher who would show me how to read, my parents thought there might be some help to be found in history. They would make me feel a part of some grand continuing thing. In 1919, I was told, the school was opened by the Prince of Wales himself (later King Edward VIII, by this time the Duke of Windsor). Great excitement was felt everywhere in this little settlement of returned soldiers, some still living in tents, some already into the tarpaper shacks they'd built while they started to clear farms out of these government-gifted parcels of stump-ridden stony land! With her piano mounted on a hay wagon, Mrs. King played "God Bless the Prince of Wales" in the open air of the schoolyard when the great moment came. But the flustered teacher discovered she'd locked the silver key inside the school. While His Royal Highness waited to do his duty and open the door, she sent a student around the back with instructions to break a window and climb inside for the key. To bring this momentous occasion to a grand finale, instead of the usual

21-gun salute, settlers dynamited 21 stumps, one after the other, and allowed His Royal Highness to set one of them off himself. Of course it was well known that immediately after this visit the Prince went missing for a couple of weeks. Buckingham Palace was frantic, the entire world was upset, but apparently we knew all along where he was – right here. Someone in our community must have caught his eye. As proof of this, I was shown a black and white snapshot of three men nailing the cedar shake roof on Elmer Sanderson's barn. One of the men was, if you squinted a bit, the smiling Prince of Wales.

But not even the Prince of Wales could soften my resolve. Not even if it could be shown that he lived here yet, incognito, and paid a daily visit to the classroom. My parents would just have to admit defeat. I was not attending school.

But neither my parents nor I had anticipated my uncle Toby's contribution to this crisis. Shortly after the prince had let my parents down, Uncle Toby and Aunt Jess and Tricia stopped by one Sunday afternoon and, of course, were invited to stay for supper along with all the others who'd just been passing by on their Sunday drive and thought it would be nice to get a breath of country air and an invitation to sample my mother's hotel-sized meals. It was during dessert that my father asked Uncle Toby if he remembered Old Four-eyes Birch.

The phrase "Do you remember . . .?" invariably had the effect of a lighted torch to the strawpile of Uncle Toby's memory. Off he immediately blazed. "Old Four-eyes? Course I remember him. Sent me a postcard once from the mental home he went to right after he taught us grade eight. He never forgot that time me'n Slim set fire to the wastepaper basket and smoked out the school like a hive of bees. He stomped his foot down into the basket to put out the flames and got it stuck. Danced around smouldering for half an hour before the janitor finally pulled it out!"

Once Uncle Toby's memory had started to blaze there was no stopping it. But like a certain type of forest fire, it roared across only the topmost branches – the surface of things – and did not take the time to burn deep.

"Remember when me'n Slim played hookey for a week and spent the time digging out under the great huge rock up the hill from the school? It rolled right down and through the front door and across the central hall and right through the wall of that pretty Miss Candle's room where she was teaching long division? You were there – tell them about the look on her face. Tell how her glasses dropped to the floor."

"How pretty was she?" my cousin Tricia asked. "What colour was her hair?"

"Remember when me'n Slim planted dynamite in the girl's privy?" said Uncle Toby. "Blew lumber and stuff as far as Sundberg's turkey farm. Some of them gobblers were nailed to the ground by falling splinters. Mrs. Drew was sneaking out for one of her secret smokes between arithmetic and art when it blew! You oughta seen that woman run! I bet she's never touched another cigarette."

Now Uncle Toby had powers even the Prince of Wales did not possess. I began to think I ought to try it out – school, that is. Not because I wanted to follow in my uncle's footsteps, but because the picture he'd left in my mind was of a school in ruins, with quivering teachers inside who were mental and physical wrecks from having to deal with the violence plotted by members of my family. I wanted to see those ruins. I wanted to see the look on some teacher's face when she heard my name and believed that another one had been sent to torment her. Even the Duke of Windsor, I believe, would not have resisted an invitation to return if he'd known all that had happened in his absence.

"Not everything your uncle Toby tells you is exactly the way it really happened," my mother said. "He's a great reader, he's always reading books – filling his head with ideas. Listening to him talk is like listening to you kids playing out in the stumps."

Maybe, I confessed to my cousin Tricia – whose hair was coming in thick and red, with even tighter curls than before I'd held a match to it – maybe it wouldn't hurt me to learn how to read a little English after all. "Not every book has pictures you can stare at."

"That's all right," she said, twisting a finger inside a tight new ringlet and looking out over the veranda rail at the rock pile and the pastures of blackened stumps. "I'll manage things around here while you're gone."

This piece was originally written for, and broadcast on, CBC Radio. It appears here in slightly shortened form.

Janice Kulyk Keefer

Novelist, poet, and critical writer, Janice Kulyk Keefer was born in Toronto and educated at the University of Toronto, and Sussex University in England.

Among the literary journals in which she has published are *Malahat*, *Descant*, *The Canadian Forum*, *NeWest Review*, and *The Antigonish Review*. In 1984, she won the Prism International Fiction Competition. In addition, she won first prize for fiction in the CBC Radio Literary Competition in 1985 and 1986, making her the first person to win twice.

Her books include *The Paris-Napoli Express* (short stories), *White of the Lesser Angels* (poetry), *Under Eastern Eyes: A Critical Reading of Maritime Fiction* (shortlisted for the Governor General's Award for 1988), and *Transfigurations* (short stories). Her first novel, *Constellations*, was published in 1988. A new collection of short stories, *Travelling Ladies*, will be published in the spring of 1990.

Janice Kulyk Keefer lives in Annapolis Royal, Nova Scotia, with her husband and two children.

JANICE KULYK KEEFER

Arks and Tunnels

I was saved by a book. Not a religious book, I hasten to add – I'm not talking about that kind of salvation. I can't remember the title, or the author's name, but in the end, that's not important. What matters is the book, the world hidden between its covers, and the doors it opened for me.

I was perhaps ten or twelve, growing up in a prosperous suburb of Toronto, and leading a life that was perfectly ordinary. That was the problem. I wanted more, I needed more than the Dick and Jane world which my schooling offered, a world in which everyone had blue eyes, a big backyard, and names like Smith or Campbell. My own last name was unpronounceable to most of my schoolmates and teachers; I might live in a split-level, yellow-brick house, but my mother had grown up in a thatched cottage with an earthen floor; my grandparents knew little English, and the stories they had to tell of their lives spoke of war, hunger, illness, exile. The knowledge that I had a foot in two worlds as unlike each other as possible bred in me an unsettling sense of difference from my peers, a difference which was a source both of vulnerability, even humiliation, and of enormous, ambitious pride. It also led to a split in my sense of who I was, and what I wanted my life to be, a split that no recourse to parents or guidance counsellors, records or television could remedy. Perhaps I didn't want to be cured of this sense of otherness, to be made "ordinary," but simply to discover ways of using difference, of exploring, understanding, and creating from it. What I did need, however, was some outside confirmation that difference, and the ambivalent feelings it produced, was a valuable part of my being; that it could empower as well as distress.

It was then, in that shaky and uncertain period of my life, that I found the book. A fortuitous find, brought about by the bookmobile that came round to our little cul-de-sac each week. There may have been the word "ark" in the title, for the book had to do with the struggles of a family to put their lives back together in a Germany that had been blown apart by World War II. It was not a happy story; there was no romance and little adventure in it, and the characters were neither heroic nor depraved. But neither were they ordinary. They were foreign – their world, their history, their society was utterly different from mine, or for that matter, from my parents – my mother's family had been lucky enough to leave Poland three years before the Nazis invaded.

The book, whatever it was called, became a passageway between my own sense of difficult difference, and a recognition of the difference of other people's lives. It also brought to me a sense of community – that I and the characters in the book, the author of the book, shared a common world much larger and more complicated than I had ever dreamed. And that I was being welcomed into another person's mind, relieved of the often unbearable loneliness of my own. What struck me most about the book, what kept me reading – and I read this book compulsively – was the honesty and acuity of the author's vision – how she saw things, what she singled out for observation, and how she let incidents and situations speak for themselves, so that I was neither bullied nor seduced by the narrative, but simply made to feel at home, to empathize or to resist according to my own ideas, my own experience.

Later, at university, I underwent another sort of crisis. First came the avalanche of despair when I realized how many books there were to be read, and how little I knew, or would ever know. And then I went through that dark, or at least sombre night of the soul which most university students experience, encountering a world of ideas so vast, complex, and contradictory that it explodes the little set of views and values on which one's childhood and adolescence are structured. This time, as well, it was a book which saw me through – not by shoring up the ruins, but rather by completing the demolition of my previous assumptions. About this book I remember specifics: it was Hermann Hesse's *Steppenwolf*. I stayed up all night reading it; I raced through each page as if it were a tunnel into a light that was dubious, and perhaps deceptive, but light, all the same. That book made me question everything I'd previously taken for granted. I wanted to throw out every possession, every bit of conceptual baggage I had acquired up till that moment, and yet I also wanted to pile those crutches high, and hide behind them. As the sun rose that morning, as the sun always does rise, even on Spadina Avenue, I felt that the floor of my life had fallen away, and that all I had to keep me from tumbling into the pit was a swaying line, no thicker than a thread. And that I had to walk it or else remain forever in a world of outgrown ideas and attitudes, of clichés and prejudices that were a worse kind of pit than anything into which reading might catapult me.

I never read anything else by Hesse – I didn't become an eastern mystic, or feel the need to slavishly adopt this writer's vision of reality. I've never reread *Steppenwolf*, partly from the fear that what I then found so extraordinarily powerful, I would now pick apart and dismiss. But the point is that I went on reading, and that for me, as for most of the people I know, not to read is to curl up and die, or at least to go into hibernation, a state all the more dangerous since there may well be no world left for us to wake up in, at all.

Literacy can be lost; those of us who, after graduation from high school or university never open any other book than the telephone directory, or even the latest Danielle Steel, are among the lost. To me, literacy means more than the ability to read manuals and signs, bank statements, or even income tax forms. It is, most important, the ability to read and to be moved by literature, which can take any form from fairy tales to the lyrics of songs. Real books – literature – rely on imagination rather than wish-fulfilment for their power, and bring us closer in some way to what is true. Truth, of course, is almost always other than what we want it to be; and as writers as varied as Henry James and Alistair MacLeod have shown, one of the most important truths we can discover is the way in which we evade or suppress knowing what we *do* know.

That very abstract term, literacy, has the connotation of bringing light into darkness, of educating millions in the third world – and thousands in our own country – who live impoverished and oppressed lives, deprived of the skills that would allow them to find the work and to assert the rights that might give them the chance for a decent and dignified life – or for life at all. Literacy for these people, whom we must consider not as "them" but as part of us, our people, means the difference between dumb endurance of intolerable hardships and the experience of living, developing one's individuality, coming to fruition as a human being. But literacy in another sense, the sense in which it affects most Canadians, is not something acquired merely to advance oneself economically or socially. Literacy – the reading of literature – is something to be valued for the complex pleasure which knowledge brings: knowing about ourselves and about others, about the world we live in, and the worlds outside to which we're all connected – South Africa, Poland, China, or perhaps Newfoundland, the B.C. interior, or Toronto's drug-bound inner city. To be truly literate is not to demand the easy satisfactions that formula romance or thrillers provide, but rather to seek out books which initiate conversations on those subjects from which we most want to hide, but about which we most need to know.

To ensure literacy, to make it flourish, we must fight for certain principles. We must oppose any government that attempts to put a tax upon reading. We must oppose sales tax on books, and any withdrawal of support from Canadian publishers and printers. In what has been called a "post-literate" age, it is becoming increasingly difficult for the printed word to make an impact on our collective consciousness – Salman Rushdie's *The Satanic Verses* notwithstanding. And that writer's tragic situation seems to me to put the case for literacy in the most pressing terms imaginable. For telling the truth as he sees it, for using the imagination to contest and satirize and also to explore a particular religion and the world view it fosters Rushdie has been made a universal scapegoat by vast numbers of people who have not even read his book. To condemn *The Satanic Verses* without having read it, and to attempt to prevent others from reading it is to deny or endanger our most precious human right – the right to know, to develop a critical understanding of whatever is presented to us as universal truth, eternal law, immutable right and wrong. The children who held up placards saying "Rushdy must Die" or "Kill the Blasfemer" are precisely the ones for whom Rushdie has written his book – the ones who, if they are to develop to their full potential as human beings, must read voraciously and omnivorously – must make up their own minds as to what is true and what false, what blasphemous and what revelatory. They must not be denied access to that process which, for example, Hermann Hesse's *Steppenwolf* began for me.

Literacy – reading – is a human right to be continuously cherished and fought for. It is not only in military dictatorships that the rights to read and to publish freely are under fire. Writers with political views considered subversive or undesirable by the powers-that-be – writers such as the distinguished linguist, Noam Chomsky, author of *The Political Economy of Human Rights* – have had enormous difficulties in getting their works published and distributed in what we like to think of as the "free world." And the increasing transformation of traditional publishing houses into offshoots of mega-corporations may well mean that fewer and fewer new, risky, alternative voices will be heard; that only what sells, and sells big, will be published. And though the Alice Munros and Margaret Atwoods are there to prove that the most accomplished literary art is compatible with the highest sales figures, one can't help anticipating that real books will be squeezed out of the publishers' lists, to be replaced by fast and phony reads – the books which do just fine on the red-eye special from Toronto to Vancouver, but which have nothing to offer when one needs something to bring one closer to life.

For there is no real polarity between books and life. Literature is a form and a way of life; it allows us to live more fully, intelligently, and honestly. And, of course, more joyfully, too. True literacy has more to do with the delights than the mechanics of reading. It is not a skill to be acquired once in a lifetime, but an art to be practised and polished one's whole life long.

JOHN FLANDERS

Award-winning novelist and poet, Joy Kogawa was born in Vancouver, B.C. Her first novel, *Obasan*, won the Books in Canada First Novel Award when it was published in Canada in 1981. Since then it has appeared in many editions, in Canada, and in the U.S., the U.K., and Japan. She wrote a children's novel, *Naomi's Road*, and her poetry books are *Splintered Moon*, *A Choice of Dreams*, *Jericho Road*, and *Woman in the Woods*.

In addition to the Books in Canada First Novel Award, Joy Kogawa has won the Canadian Authors Association Book of the Year Award, the Best Paperback Fiction Award from the Periodical Distributors of Canada, the American Book Award, the American Library Association's Notable Book Prize, and she has been made a Member of the Order of Canada.

She has been director of the Canadian Civil Liberties Association, and is a member of the Writers' Union of Canada and PEN International.

Joy Kogawa lives in Toronto, where she is completing her next novel.

JOY KOGAWA

Where There's a Wall

where there's a wall
there's a way
around, over, or through
there's a gate
maybe a ladder
a door
a sentinel who sometimes sleeps
there are secret passwords
you can overhear
there are methods of torture
for extracting clues
to maps of underground passageways
there are zeppelins
helicopters, rockets, bombs
battering rams
armies with trumpets
whose all at once blast
shatters the foundations

where there's a wall
there are words
to whisper by a loose brick
wailing prayers to utter
special codes to tap
birds to carry messages
taped to their feet
there are letters to be written
novels even

on this side of the wall
I am standing staring at the top
lost in clouds
I hear every sound to make
but cannot see you

I incline in the wrong direction
a voice cries faint as in a dream
from the belly
of the wall

"Where There's a Wall" was originally published in *Woman in the Woods* (Mosaic Press, 1985), and appears here in revised form. Reprinted with permission.

Ant and Bee Poem

Love, I say meaning
glue, as in I
glue you to
everything – the
sky, the kitchen
cupboard. I glue you
to this letter that
I seal with moist
tongue and Love,
I say, meaning
food, as in
send me your
round nubby words
to taste, the sweet
chewy texture of
honeycomb wax
and Love, I say,
meaning hunger and
this flung apart
longing and the busy
ants on the cupboard wall
carrying bits of sweet wax
home.

"Ant and Bee Poem" originally appeared in *Woman in the Woods* (Mosaic Press, 1985). Reprinted with permission.

Gordon Korman was born October 23, 1963 in Montreal, Quebec, and moved with his family to the Toronto area in 1971. He was twelve years old when he wrote his first book, *This Can't Be Happening at Macdonald Hall*, as a Grade 7 English assignment. It was published by Scholastic, and, at age fourteen, Gordon Korman was a best-selling author. Now, some dozen or so books later, Gordon holds a Fine Arts degree from New York University, with a major in Dramatic and Visual writing, and a minor in Motion Picture and Television. His recent books include: *Son of Interflux*, *A Semester in the Life of a Garbage Bag*, *The Zucchini Warriors*, *Radio 5th Grade*, *Losing Joe's Place* (a Young Adult novel). He is a member of The Canadian Society of Children's Authors, Illustrators and Performers, The Writers' Union of Canada, The Canadian Authors Association, The Society of Children's Book Writers (U.S.) and ACTRA, and his books have won awards and recognition both in Canada and the U.S.

GORDON KORMAN

Don't Wait for the Movie

I remember a conversation with a producer who was working on turning one of my books into a feature film. The more I heard, the more I became convinced that I had better savour the moment when "Based on the Novel by . . ." flashed on the screen, because it was going to be the only thing in the movie even vaguely reminiscent of what I wrote.

I think it finally sank in when the producer said, "Well, you know the scene where Steve –?"

"Wait a second," I interrupted. "Who's Steve?"

How ignorant of me to think that, as the guy who wrote the book, I should actually be able to recognize the hero, especially after they plotted, replotted, unplotted, added, excised, and replaced personnel like Harold Ballard. Can't tell the players without a scorecard.

Then I thought of the junior high school student who might someday be called upon to do a book report on my book. He would plow over to the video store to rent *that* movie, save time, and come up with a report destined to flunk with flying colours. (The character sketch of Steve would lay a particularly large egg.) Every one of us has beaten a deadline by condensing a lot of reading time into a 90-minute movie.

All this is hypothetical, of course, because the proposed movie never got made – which is why I am not dictating this piece over the cellular phone in my Maserati. But it did get me thinking about book versus movie, and what makes a book so special, since it obviously isn't time efficiency.

Lately, teachers have thrown us a curve. Now we have to read the book *and* see the movie, and compare the two. Teachers are very big on comparisons. Here it works. Almost invariably, the book gets the nod.

That's not to say that all the movies are bad. After the books, though, they're just somehow incomplete. The novel always seems to have something more – a greater depth, a different perspective, a more incisive insight and humour. There is something unique to the written word – to that relationship between author and reader – which cannot be reproduced any other way. It's more than just reporting or storytelling. It's *different*.

A reader participates in a novel. In a sense, it is almost a collaboration between him and the writer as, reading, he supplies his own interpretation – the reader's draft. No two are ever alike. You can read the same book as someone else without reading the same book. (For instance, everybody who read *Lord Jim* and liked it read a different book than I did. That may be because I'm a poor "collaborator" with Joseph Conrad.) There is a feeling of accomplishment when you come to the end of a very good book – you have completed a successful collaboration. Don't expect royalties.

This is all coming from someone who was a staunch non-reader in elementary school. Once, in a book report, just to avoid actually reading anything, I went so far as to make up an entire novel, characters and all, using my friend's kid sister as the writer. There was even a section on "other books by the same author," and an excerpt from the *Boston Globe* review. It took ten times as much energy as doing the assignment properly, but to me, no amount of figuring the angles was unjustified. I didn't want to read, period. I got an A. Crime pays.

What finally hooked me in was humour. When I found books that made me laugh, my sense of the "work" of reading was replaced by something wonderful and totally unfamiliar – a desire to find out what happened next. It was a crucial connection. From then on, I equated reading with enjoying myself, and I was a reader for good.

This may sound like an oversimplification, but beware. Relating reading and enjoyment can't be taught; it has to happen. It's a click. Without that click, no amount of explanation, no pleading, no assurance that this is a "great story," will do any good. In my case, humour produced the desired click. But mystery, suspense, adventure, science-fiction, romance, and nonfiction can do the job too. I tend to stick with the funny stuff as the best bet. Tastes can be very specialized, but just about everybody loves to laugh.

My father used to summarize his reading history with the statement, "I read a book once," which was, unfortunately, not greatly exaggerated. Then, out of parental loyalty, he started reading my work. But when I didn't seem to be churning them out fast enough, he tried other authors, and found that you don't have to be a blood relative to appreciate good writing. Now it's not uncommon to find him with a good book in his hand. Reading helps you develop a facility for language, which in turn helps you to read. A neat circle.

Being literate, by definition, is being able to read and write and function in society with these acquired skills. After that, you're on your own, and your reading is what you yourself choose to make of it. Education and reading material are abundant in Canada, and sharing with the rest of the world is something we are fortunate to be able to do. But we, who have all the advantages, often lack something the disadvantaged have to a man – motivation. Too many of our kids don't *want* to read. They equate reading exclusively with work and school – something that is done only under duress, never voluntarily. I had one childhood friend whose parents actually used it as punishment; the greater the infraction, the more days he would have to spend reading. I've lost touch with him, but I'm pretty sure he reads nothing to this day. Would you?

We have to play up the entertainment side of reading as our kids take their first step towards books. If they latch onto a topic that grabs them, the books will do the rest. Then, in the all-important war for rapidly dwindling leisure time, reading will have a fighting chance with the big boys – hockey, MuchMusic, *Friday the 13th: Part 173*, and Super Mega-Deluxe Mario Brothers 40. We don't have to wipe out the competition (we haven't got a prayer, and we shouldn't want to) but it would be nice to be on the program.

I once got a letter from a ten-year-old boy who wrote: "I hate reading, but your books are different. I'm going to read them all." It was not only flattering and good business, but also encouraging. I *know* that kid will discover, as he develops the reading habit with my stuff, a lot of other authors who are "different," and that he'll go on to be a real reader.

Chalk one up for our side.

JOHN FOLEY

Internationally acclaimed novelist and poet, Michael Ondaatje was born in Sri Lanka, where his family had lived for several generations. He left there at the age of eleven to go to school in England. He came to Canada in 1962. He has published *The Dainty Monsters*, *The Man with 7 Toes*, *Rat Jelly*, *Running in the Family*, and *Secular Love*. In addition, in 1970, his book of poetry and prose called *The Collected Works of Billy the Kid* was published and won the Governor General's Award. *Coming through Slaughter*, published in 1976, won the Books in Canada First Novel Award. *There's a Trick with a Knife I'm Learning to Do* won the Governor General's Award in 1980. Stage versions of *The Collected Works of Billy the Kid* and *Coming through Slaughter* have been produced in Canada and abroad.

Originally published in Canada, where it won The Trillium Award and The City of Toronto Book Award, his latest novel, *In the Skin of a Lion*, has received high praise internationally. It has been published in many editions in the U.S., the U.K., and Canada, and in translation in France, Italy, Sweden, Holland, Spain, and Denmark.

Michael Ondaatje lives in Toronto, where he teaches at Glendon College, York University.

MICHAEL ONDAATJE

from *In the Skin of a Lion*

The event that will light the way for immigration in North America is the talking picture. The silent film brings nothing but entertainment – a pie in the face, a fop being dragged by a bear out of a department store – all events governed by fate and timing, not language and argument. The tramp never changes the opinion of the policeman. The truncheon swings, the tramp scuttles through a corner window and disturbs the fat lady's ablutions. These comedies are nightmares. The audience emits horrified laughter as Chaplin, blindfolded, rollerskates near the edge of the unbalconied mezzanine. No one shouts to warn him. He cannot talk or listen. North America is still without language, gestures and work and bloodlines are the only currency.

But it was a spell of language that brought Nicholas here, arriving in Canada without a passport in 1914, a great journey made in silence.

* * *

He took a train for Toronto where there were many from his village; he would not be among strangers. But there was no work. So he took a train north to Copper Cliff, near Sudbury, and worked there in a Macedonian bakery. He was paid seven dollars a month with food and sleeping quarters. After six months he went to Sault Ste. Marie. He still could hardly speak English and decided to go to school, working nights in another Macedonian bakery. If he did not learn the language he would be lost.

The school was free. The children in the class were ten years old and he was twenty-six. He used to get up at two in the morning and make dough and bake until 8:30. At nine he would go to school. The teachers were all young ladies and were very good people. During this time in the Sault he had translation dreams – because of his fast and obsessive studying of English. In the dreams trees changed not just their names but their looks and character. Men started answering in falsettos. Dogs spoke out fast to him as they passed him on the street.

When he returned to Toronto all he needed was a voice for all this language. Most immigrants learned their English from recorded songs or, until the talkies came, through mimicking actors on stage. It was a common habit to select one actor and follow him throughout his career, annoyed when he was given a small part, and seeing each of his plays as often as possible – sometimes as often as ten times during a run. Usually by the end of an east-end production at the Fox or Parrot Theatres the actors' speeches would be followed by growing echoes as Macedonians, Finns, and Greeks repeated the phrases after a half-second pause, trying to get the pronunciation right.

This infuriated the actors, especially when a line such as "Who put the stove in the living room, Kristin?" – which had originally brought the house down – was now spoken simultaneously by at least seventy people and so tended to lose its spontaneity. When the matinee idol Wayne Burnett dropped dead during a performance, a Sicilian butcher took over, knowing his lines and his blocking meticulously, and money did not have to be refunded.

Certain actors were popular because they spoke slowly. Lethargic ballads, and a kind of blues where the first line of a verse is repeated three times, were in great demand. Sojourners walked out of their accent into regional American voices. Nicholas Temelcoff, unfortunately, would later choose Fats Waller as his model and so his emphasis on usually unnoticed syllables and the throwaway lines made him seem high-strung or dangerously anti-social or too loving.

But during the time he worked on the bridge, he was seen as a recluse. He would begin sentences in his new language, mutter, and walk away. He became a vault of secrets and memories. Privacy was the only weight he carried. None of his cohorts really knew him. This man, awkward in groups, would walk off and leave strange clues about himself, like a dog's footprints on the snowed roof of a garage.

Excerpted from *In the Skin of a Lion*, which was originally published by McClelland & Stewart Inc., 1987. Reprinted by permission.

MARTIN SLEWELLING

Highly acclaimed fiction writer David Adams Richards was born in Newcastle, New Brunswick, in 1950. His first novel, *The Coming of Winter* was awarded the Norma Epstein Prize, and also appeared in translation in Russia. His other novels are: *Blood Ties*, *Lives of Short Duration*, *Road to the Stilt House*, and *Nights Below Station Street*, which won the Governor General's Award for Fiction (1988). From 1983 to 1987, Richards was writer-in-residence at the University of New Brunswick. In 1986, he was named one of Canada's Ten Best Fiction Writers, in the "45 Below" competition. In January 1990, he was profiled in *Maclean's* magazine's "Honor Role" of twelve Canadians whose accomplishments "made a difference" in 1989.

David Adams Richards lives with his wife, Peggy, and their baby son, John Thomas, in Saint John, New Brunswick. He has just completed, for the CBC, the screenplay for a film version of *Nights Below Station Street*. His next novel will be published in the fall of 1990.

DAVID ADAMS RICHARDS

Illiteracy: A Personal Perspective

This is a true story about my godchild.

He is fairly ordinary. Bright, tough, and good-hearted. He has a good memory. For example, a lover of hockey and baseball, he can remember the number or name of a player after hearing it once. He remembers where and when a player was traded, who was traded for him, and why the deal was made.

In games he is clumsy – but a dedicated and fierce opponent. It goes against his nature to give in.

To him this story would not be significant. I suppose he wouldn't look at it the way I do at all – just as my great-uncle, who never learned to read or write, might not understand how humbled I was when, forgetting myself, I asked him how long a canoe he helped build was. He looked at me sheepishly a moment, looked at the canoe, and then proudly said, "She's long enough, I guess."

My godchild was also determined to find ways around questions. At school he was average, or better. But he did disturb the class now and again by talking out loud and singing, getting up and scratching his bum, or, now and then, rolling down the aisle in a wrestling match; all those things we should all be allowed to do anyway. (And how can you disrupt kids who always love to be, and go out of their way to be, disrupted?)

Sometimes, when he was quite small, he had to be tied to his bed with a fishnet so he wouldn't get up in the middle of the night and climb up on the roof. To make this point a little clearer: some friends of mine were walking home from the bar at two in the morning and saw this little fellow, sitting on the highest eave of the house, waving at them in pajamas and gumboots.

To him, it was clear. He wanted to do it – he never thought of falling.

So as I have said, he is a fairly ordinary boy of about four-foot something. And he started the fourth year of school without much fanfare. But unfortunately, things were not all that they seemed.

I guess there were just too many traps laid out for him. Nobody knew they were traps, except himself. He knew they were traps but he could tell no-one about them. So we could not help him. He had to dodge them, think of ways to get around them by himself. That he did it for so long is a measure of his ultimate triumph, the true measure of his intelligence.

Things started to close in after a while though, about October of that year. Too many pages piled up, too many words had to be kept in place. Finally one day at school he had to answer too many questions.

At first, he denied he couldn't read, surprised it had all ended at the principal's office one rainy autumn afternoon.

If was as if he knew those words of advice: "Don't complain – don't explain – and if worse comes to worse – sue."

So he denied it all. And kept looking from one to the other and back again, as if for help.

But the proof was against him. The evidence had piled up over the three years. They finally had him dead to rights. He was nine years old, had begun grade four and could not read. The real surprise was, no-one, not even his teachers or his parents, had known it for this long.

He fooled everyone. He had never mastered the alphabet because of a learning disability, a part of the very hyperactiveness which caused him to climb upon the roof at night, waving nonchalantly to those below.

It almost seemed impossible to him to learn how to read. So, without complaining, he had done what was second nature to him. He had memorized what to read. And wherever the teachers or other students said the words went on the page, that was good enough for him.

It worked well – for a while. Even his teachers, though occasionally baffled by him, did not catch on.

He had managed this task by sheer tenacity and raw intelligence.

But it didn't matter – once found out, he believed he was stupid. Since he hadn't wanted to let anyone know he was stupid, he had memorized three readers by rote and was working on his fourth. He kept the secret to himself.

Whenever he was asked to read, one teacher has said: "He would stand up and give the performance of his life."

At nine years of age I'm sure he believed his life depended on it.

It was overwhelming odds, all right. But it almost worked. So God bless him. A strange testimony to the courage of the human spirit.

My great uncle had to leave school in grade three. He swept the church steps and shovelled snow off the sidewalk for parishioners, removed his hat in front of ladies, and would not smoke in their presence. He would not understand that this is now considered quaint and anachronistic.

My godchild has a tutor. His learning disability is being overcome, and he is learning to read what he had once memorized with such facility.

Ben Wicks

Ben Wicks was born in London, England, and came to Canada in 1957. In 1960, his first cartoons were accepted by *The Saturday Evening Post*. He joined the *Toronto Telegram* in 1962, and the *Los Angeles Times* syndicated his work in 1964. As a journalist, he covered the war in Biafra for the *Los Angeles Times and Telegram*. He has written for the *London Sunday Times*, the *London Observer*, the *New York Daily News*, and the *American Medical Journal*. He lived with the rebels of Eritrea, Northern Ethiopia, while covering the war for *The Toronto Star* in 1985. He has travelled to the Sudan to cover the refugee situation, Haiti, the coup in Uganda, and to other areas of the world. A television program for the CBC network, "The World of Wicks," ran for six years. He now writes a regular column, "Wicks," for *The Toronto Star*. In 1987, the Governor General of Canada presented Ben Wicks with the Order of Canada.

Ben Wicks lives in Toronto.

What if it says 'No dogs'?

PHILIP MARTIN

Acclaimed as one of Canada's foremost novelists, Rudy Wiebe was born in 1934 and grew up on a Mennonite homestead in Saskatchewan. He published his first novel in 1962 and received the Governor General's Award for Fiction in 1973 for *The Temptations of Big Bear*. Wiebe has published nineteen books, comprising fiction, nonfiction, and drama. Many are based on the people and history of western Canada. His works include: *The Mad Trapper*, *The Angel of the Tar Sands*, *The Scorched-Wood People*, *Peace Shall Destroy Many*, and *My Lovely Enemy*. His most recent book is *Playing Dead: A Contemplation Concerning the Arctic*.

Rudy Wiebe lives in Edmonton.

RUDY WIEBE

Speaking Saskatchewan

In summer the thick green poplar leaves clicked and flickered at him, in winter the stiff spruce rustled with voices. The boy, barefoot in the heat or trussed up like a lumpy package against the fierce, silver cold, went alone to the bush where everything spoke: the warm rocks, the flit of quick, small animals, a dart of birds, tree trunks, burning air, ground, the squeaky snow: everything as he breathed and became aware, its language clear as the water of his memory when he lay in the angle of the house rafters at night listening to the mosquitoes slowly find him under his blanket, though he had his eyes shut and only one ear uncovered. Everything spoke, and it spoke Low German.

Like his mother. She would call him long, long into the summer evening when it seemed the sun burned all night down into the north, call long and slow as if she were already weeping and when he appeared beside her she would bend her wide powerful hands about his head and kiss him so hard his eyes rang. "Why don't you answer, you?" she would speak against his hair. "Why don't you ever answer when I call, it's so dark, why don't you ever say a word?" While he nuzzled his face into the damp apron at the fold of her thigh, and soon her words would be over and he heard her skin and warm apron smelling of saskatoon jam and dishes and supper buns love him back.

His sister laughed at his solitary silence. "In school are thirty kids," she would say, "you'll have to talk, and English at that. You can't say Low German there, and if you don't answer English when she asks, the teacher will make you stand in the corner."

"Right in front, of people?" he would ask fearfully.

'Yeah, in front of every one of them, your face against the wall. So you better start to talk, English too."

And she would try to teach him English names for things, but he did not listen to that. Rather, when he was alone he practised standing in the corners of walls. Their logs shifted and cracked, talking. Walls were very good, especially where they came together so warm in winter.

But outside was even better, and he followed a quiet trail of the muskrat that had dented the snow with its tail between bullrushes sticking out of the slough ice, or waited for the coyote to turn and see him, its paw lifted and about to touch a drift, its jaw opening on a red tongue laughing with him. In summer he heard a mother bear talk to her cubs among the willows of the horse pasture, though he did not see them, but he found their sluffing paw prints in the spring snow and his father said something would have to be done if they came that close to the pig fence again. The boy knew his father refused to own a gun, but their nearest neighbour west gladly hunted everywhere to shoot whatever he heard about and so he folded his hands over the huge, wet prints and whispered in Low German, "Don't visit here any more. It's dangerous."

The school sat on the corner, just below the hill where the road turned south along the creek to the church and the store. He never looked at the school, the tiny panes of its four huge windows staring at him, just staring. The day before he had to go there every day like his sister, the planes came for the first time.

Their horses were pulling the wagon up the hill as slowly, steadily as they always did and it happened very fast, almost before he looked around. There had been a rumble from somewhere like thunder, far away, though the sky was clear sunlight and his father had just said in a week they could start bindering the oats, it was ripening so well, and his mother sat beside him broad and straight as always, her braided, waist-long hair coiled up for church under her hat when the roaring planes were there as he turned, four, yellow-and-black, louder than anything he had ever heard. West over the school and the small grain fields and pastures and all the trees and hills to the far edge of the world. His father would not look around, holding the horses in carefully, muttering, "Now it comes here too, that war training," but the boy was looking at his mother. Perhaps his own face looked like that next morning when the yellow planes came over the school at recess, so low he saw huge glass eyes in a horrible leather head glare down at him before he screamed and ran inside to the desk where his sister had said he must sit. When he opened his eyes the face of the teacher was there, her gentle face very close, smiling almost up-side-down at him between the iron legs of the desk beneath which he crouched. Her gentle voice.

"Come," she said, "come," and after a moment he scrambled to his feet; he thought she was speaking Low German because he did not yet know that what that word meant was spoken the same in English. Not touching him, she led him between desks to a cupboard against the wall opposite the windows and opened its narrow door. Books. He has never imagined so many books. There may be a million.

She is, of course, speaking to him in English and later, when he remembers that moment again and again, he will never be able to explain how he can understand what she is saying. The open book in her hand shows him countless words: words, she tells him, he can now only see the shape of, but he will be able to hear them when he learns to read, and that the word "READ" in English is the same as the word "SPEAK," *raed*, in Low German and through reading all the people of the world will speak to him from books, when he reads he will be able to hear them, and he will understand. He is staring at what he later knows are a few worn books on a few shelves, and then staring back at the few visible but as yet unintelligible words revealed in her hand, and slowly he understands that there are shelves and shelves of books in great stacks on many, many floors inside all the walls of the enormous libraries of the world where he will go and read: where the knowing she will now help him discover within himself will allow him to listen to human voices speaking from everywhere and every age, saying everything, things both dreadful and beautiful, and all that can be imagined between them; and that he will listen. He will listen to those voices speaking now for as long as he lives.